United Nations
vs Israel

and the End of the World

www.UNvsIL.com

". . . all the nations on earth will come together to attack Jerusalem."
—Zechariah 12:3 NCV

David A. Reed

To my wife, whose inner and outward beauty is,
for me, sufficient proof of the existence of God

September 6, 2012

www.UNvsIL.com

Books by David A. Reed include:
Jehovah's Witnesses Answered Verse by Verse
Answering Jehovah's Witnesses Subject by Subject
Mormons Answered Verse by Verse
Parallel Gospels in Harmony - with Study Guide
Come, Follow Jesus! (the real Jesus)

United Nations vs Israel and the End of the World

ISBN-13: 978-1478213130

ISBN-10: 1478213132

Scripture References

Unless otherwise noted, Scripture quoted in this book is from the World English Bible, a copyright-free translation in the public domain.
LB   The Living Bible © 1971 by Tyndale House Publishers
NASB   New American Standard Bible © 1995 by Lockman Foundation
NCV   The Holy Bible, New Century Version © 2005 by Thomas Nelson, Inc.
NEB   New English Bible © 1961, 1970 by Oxford University Press and Cambridge University Press
NIV   The Holy Bible, New International Version © 1973, 1978, 1984 by International Bible Society
NKJV   New King James Version, Holy Bible © 1983 by Thomas Nelson, Inc.
NLT   New Living Translation © 1996, 2004, 2007 by Tyndale House Publishers
RSV   Revised Standard Version © 1946, 1952 by Division of Christian Education of the Churches of Christ in the United States of America

Contents

The Nations Uniting against Israel
Signals the End of the World

Several ancient Bible prophecies about Israel and Jerusalem have already come true in recent decades, including the foretold restoration of the Jewish state and Jewish control over Jerusalem. The remaining prophecies point to an international confrontation over Jerusalem that will lead to the battle of Armageddon, the return of Christ, and the end of the world.

First, according to these prophecies, Jerusalem would become a problem for the whole world. And then the nations would unite in an attempt to enforce a solution:

"Jerusalem will be a heavy stone burdening the world . . . all the nations of the earth unite in an attempt . . ." — Zechariah 12:3 LB

United Nations resolutions quoted later in this book show that the international community today does view Jerusalem as a problem for the whole world. And these U.N. resolutions form a legal basis for the international community to take concerted military action. Soon, as the Bible says,

". . . all the nations on earth will come together to attack Jerusalem." —Zechariah 12:3 NCV

"They . . . go out to all the rulers of the world to gather them for battle . . . all the rulers and their armies to a place with the Hebrew name [Armageddon]" [a location in Israel]. —Revelation 16:14-16 NLT

Yes, the Bible makes it plain that the restoration of Jewish control over the land of Israel and Jerusalem would lead up to military action against Israel by the rest of the world. The prophet Joel quotes God as saying this:

"'At that time, when I restore the prosperity of Judah and Jerusalem,' says the LORD, 'I will gather the armies of the world into the valley of Jehoshaphat'" [a location in Israel]. —Joel 3:1-2 NLT

And this military action would be met by Divine intervention:

"The armies of heaven . . . defeat the nations"

—Revelation 19:14-15 NCV

"The God of heaven will set up another kingdom that will . . . crush all the other kingdoms and bring them to an end . . ."

—Daniel 2:44 NCV

This book does not endorse the policies of the Israeli government. Rather, it points out Bible prophecies that condemn Israel. But the prophecies also cite Israel and Jerusalem as a timeline marker and as a warning for all mankind.

Some two thousand years after Roman legions destroyed ancient Jerusalem and scattered the Jewish people worldwide, the state of Israel was restored with Jerusalem as its capital—against all odds, but exactly as predicted in the Bible.

So, what about the remaining prophecies that all the nations will unite against Israel, mobilize armies against Jerusalem, and march into the war of Armageddon that will end the world as we know it? The prophecies that have already been fulfilled guarantee that the rest will also come true.

As this book will demonstrate, the Hebrew Old Testament and the Greek New Testament both contain prophecies pointing to the same series of events. Written by different human penmen, but inspired by the same God, these prophecies agree that the world's governments will unite to mobilize their armed forces against Israel, just before God brings an end to this world.

What else does the Bible say about the time period leading up to the end?

It would be a time when environmental disasters would plague mankind. The prophecies mention earthquakes in one place after another:

". . . earthquakes in various places."

—Matthew 24:7 NCV

There would be destructive ocean waves like those caused recently by severe coastal storms and devastating tsunamis:

". . . distress of nations in perplexity at the roaring of the sea and the waves . . ."

—Luke 21:25 RSV

Mankind would be plagued by climate change with extreme weather events:

". . . and the sun was given power to scorch people with fire. They were seared by the intense heat. . ."

—Revelation 16:8-9 NIV

Like the volcanic eruptions that have interfered with air traffic in recent years, smoke rising up from beneath the earth would plague mankind:

"When he opened the Abyss, smoke rose from it like the smoke from a gigantic furnace."

—Revelation 9:2

The prophecies foretell drastic deforestation world wide:

". . . one third of the trees were burnt up . . ."

—Revelation 8:7

And the planet's sea life would be threatened, with fish stocks greatly reduced, much as we see happening in the world today:

". . . a third of the living creatures in the sea died . . ."

—Revelation 8:8-9

The prophecies of the end of the world also point to the immoral cities of Sodom and Gomorrah as examples of what will happen to this world:

". . . the evil cities of Sodom and Gomorrah . . . an example of what is going to happen to those who are against God."

—2 Peter 2:6 NCV

The prophecies go on to say worldwide opposition to Israel will culminate in the final war of Armageddon that will destroy all human governments. The government of the United States will cease to exist. The governments of the European Union countries will fall. The government of the state of Israel will be replaced. And most of the people on earth will be killed in the final war that these prophecies describe. But those who survive will find peace and happiness under a new world government ruled by Jesus, the Messiah.

So, our survival and the future of our loved ones depend on how we prepare now for what is coming.

This book explains what these ancient prophecies actually say, how today's events are already lining up with what was foretold—as well as what you need to do to survive. Gaining life in the peaceful new world that will replace this evil world is not a matter of chance or of survival skills. Rather, it is a matter of following the instructions found in the Scriptures alongside these prophecies, as this book will discuss.

Bible Prophecies Don't Endorse
Israel's Behavior

Do the Bible prophecies about Israel and Jerusalem mean that God endorses the government of Israel and its policies? No!—not at all.

The Bible makes mention of Israel from nearly beginning to end, as a warning example for the rest of mankind:

"Now these things happened as examples for us, so that we would not crave evil things as they also craved. Do not be idolaters, as some of them were . . . Nor let us act immorally, as some of them did . . . Nor let us try the LORD, as some of them did . . . Nor grumble, as some of them did . . . Now these things happened to them as an example, and they were written for our instruction, upon whom the ends of the ages have come."

—1 Corinthians 10:6-11 NIV

The ancient nation of Israel was blessed when it obeyed God's instructions, and it was cursed when it disobeyed.

"The Israelites quit following the LORD and worshiped Baal and Ashtoreth. The LORD was angry with the people of Israel, so he handed them over to robbers who took their possessions. He let their enemies who lived around them defeat them; they could not protect themselves. When the Israelites went out to fight, they always lost, because the LORD was not with them. The LORD had sworn to them this would happen. So the Israelites suffered very much."

—Judges 2:13-15 NCV

Although Israel had a few good leaders over the centuries, the Bible condemns most of the kings of Israel as evil:

"Jehoram was thirty and two years old when he began to reign; and he reigned eight years in Jerusalem . . . and he did that which was evil in the sight of the LORD."

—2 Chronicles 21:5-6 The Holy Scriptures,
Jewish Publication Society of America

7

"Forty and two years old was Ahaziah when he began to reign; and he reigned one year in Jerusalem . . . And he did that which was evil in the sight of the LORD."

—2 Chronicles 22:2-4 The Holy Scriptures
Jewish Publication Society of America

Similar condemnation is recorded for most of the kings who ruled in Jerusalem, and for most of the Jewish kings who ruled in Samaria over the breakaway northern kingdom of Israel. They followed policies that were displeasing to God, for the most part, and they were condemned for it in the Bible.

So, the fact that Shimon Peres or Ariel Sharon or Ehud Olmert or Benjamin Netanyahu or some other politician might be ruling as prime minister of Israel does not mean that their governmental policies are God's chosen policies.

Rather, the government of modern Israel is included when the prophecies state that God will replace all human governments:

". . . the God of heaven will set up another kingdom that will never be destroyed or given to another group of people. This kingdom will crush all the other kingdoms and bring them to an end, but it will continue forever."

—Daniel 2:44 NCV

Messiah's kingdom will restore justice and fairness to government and will finally bring peace to this planet, in a way that human governments have never been able to do.

"The Spirit of the LORD will rest upon that king. . . . This king will be glad to obey the LORD. He will not judge by the way things look or decide by what he hears. But he will judge the poor honestly; he will be fair in his decisions for the poor people of the land."

—Isaiah 11:2-4 NCV

This king who will rule the earth after the coming war of Armageddon is Jesus of Nazareth, the Jewish Messiah, who rose from the dead and promised to return in power. (The word *Messiah* comes from the Hebrew language and means *anointed ruler*. The word *Christ* comes from the Greek language and means the same thing.) In contrast with the present rulers of Israel—and the leaders of other nations—the Scriptures reveal Jesus to be kind, compassionate and merciful:

"'Come to me, all you who labor and are heavily burdened, and I will give you rest.

"'Take my yoke upon you, and learn from me, for I am gentle and lowly in heart; and you will find rest for your souls.

"'For my yoke is easy, and my burden is light.'"   —Matthew 11:28-30

Only a minority of Jews in the first century accepted Jesus' invitation to become his followers. Their religious and political leaders were jealous of him and handed him over to the occupying forces of the Roman Empire for execution as a criminal. He died a sacrificial death for the sins of his people and for the sins of the whole world—as foretold in the Hebrew Scriptures. But God raised him from the dead on the third day, as also foretold. Jesus then appeared alive to his followers on a number of occasions.

"Then he opened their minds so they could understand the Scriptures. He told them, 'This is what is written: The Messiah will suffer and rise from the dead on the third day, and repentance for the forgiveness of sins will be preached in his name to all nations, beginning at Jerusalem.'"

—Luke 24:45-47 NIV

He also told them what to do while waiting for him to return in power:

"'All power in heaven and on earth is given to me. So go and make followers of all people in the world. Baptize them in the name of the Father and the Son and the Holy Spirit. Teach them to obey everything that I have taught you, and I will be with you always, even until the end of this age.'"   —Matthew 28:18-20 NCV

All power in heaven and on earth has been given to Jesus the Messiah. When he returns, his Kingdom government will replace not only the present government of Israel, but also the governments of all the nations on earth.

As Foretold, the Nations Are Already United and Prepared to Act

How realistic is it to think of the nations of today's world uniting to deal with the problem of Jerusalem, and to impose an international solution by military force? Although people may not be generally aware of it, events have been moving in that direction for decades.

Back in 1947, the nations of the world debated how to divide British-ruled Palestine into two states—one Arab and the other Jewish. The nations decided that Jerusalem would sit between the two new countries, and that neither one of them would control the city. The General Assembly of the United Nations passed its Resolution 181, which was voted on and approved on November 29 of that year. Section C of Part II of that Resolution was titled "The City of Jerusalem" and, in effect, claimed the authority of the United Nations to determine and establish "the boundaries of the City of Jerusalem." General Assembly Resolution 181, Part III, Section A, stated that the city must not be part of the state of Israel, nor part of any Arab state. Rather, it must be an "international" city administered by the United Nations.

Representing the nations of the whole world, the General Assembly declared:

"The City of Jerusalem shall be established as a corpus separatum under a special international regime and shall be administered by the United Nations. The Trusteeship Council shall be designated to discharge the responsibilities of the Administering Authority on behalf of the United Nations."

And in Section B titled "Boundaries of the City" U. N. General Assembly Resolution 181 went on to specify that

"The City of Jerusalem shall include the present municipality of Jerusalem plus the surrounding villages and towns."

More recently in the year 2002, the "Quartet" composed of the United States, Russia, the European Union and the United Nations drew up a "roadmap for peace" and presented it formally to the government of Israel and to the Palestinian Authority in May, 2003. That roadmap envisions, in its final phase of implementation, an international conference to achieve

"resolution on the status of Jerusalem that takes into account the political and religious concerns of both sides, and protects the religious interests of Jews, Christians and Muslims worldwide."

Later chapters of this book will look more closely at this and subsequent resolutions regarding the status of Jerusalem passed by both the General Assembly and the Security Council of the United Nations, and at the Quartet's roadmap for peace. But this much is mentioned here to demonstrate that "all the nations of the earth" have already started to "unite in an attempt" to impose their solution for the problem posed by Jerusalem. (Zechariah 12:3 *The Living Bible*)

Besides simply drawing up resolutions on Jerusalem and voting to make them official, the international community also seems to be moving in the direction of enforcing those resolutions. According to a report in the *Jerusalem Post Internet Edition,* British Foreign Secretary Jack Straw said, "the West has been guilty of double standards—on the one hand saying the UN Security Council resolutions on Iraq must be implemented, on the other hand, sometimes appearing rather quixotic over the implementation of resolutions about Israel and Palestine." (From the article titled, "Foreign Ministry slams British PM's linkage of Iraq, Intifada," by Douglas Davis, March 26, 2003)

The same article quoted British Prime Minister Tony Blair as saying that the American President George W. Bush "believes, like me, that this is a vital interest to resolve because it is probably the issue, more than anything else, that keeps the Arab and Muslim worlds and the Western world apart." Prime Minister Blair spoke those words less than a week after the British armed forces had entered active combat, alongside American forces, with the stated goal of enforcing Security Council resolutions on Iraq.

Linking "the implementation of resolutions about Israel and Palestine" to the military enforcement of resolutions about Iraq carries ominous implications, and, not surprisingly, the British statements drew strong criticism from the Israeli government.

Is the world really moving toward a head-on conflict with God? Israeli-Palestinian talks broke down in the year 2000, with neither side willing to yield on the status of Jerusalem. The violence and terror that followed hit Israel first, but then spread worldwide. The attack of September 11, 2001 brought the conflict to America. Now, fear of terrorism grips the world. Much of the world also lives in fear of the American military response that was demonstrated first in Afghanistan and then in Iraq. World public opinion rages against these American actions and against the Israeli military actions in Gaza and the West Bank. As tensions rise between Muslim nations and the West, many point to the violence in and around Jerusalem as the root cause.

While radical Islamic leaders enlist followers to 'march on Jerusalem,' other diplomats advocate placing Jerusalem under international control, policed by United Nations peacekeeping forces. The government of Israel has been following such talk, of course, and has long been resolved to hold onto Jerusalem at all costs.

The Jerusalem Post Internet Edition carried a story by Gil Hoffman on November 7, 2001, reporting, "The diplomatic plan that Foreign Minister Shimon Peres is formulating with Prime Minister Ariel Sharon is intended to prevent the international community from imposing its own plans on Israel, Sharon explained yesterday." That same report added these details: "Explaining the urgency of the Sharon-Peres diplomatic initiative, the Foreign Minister referred to plans circulating out of the United States, European Union, and United Nations and said that Israel cannot let its actions be driven by the agendas of other bodies with vested interests." (The *Jerusalem Post*'s internet edition can be found online at www.jpost.com.)

So, Israeli politicians see the possibility of 'the international community imposing' a solution, and they are determined to resist. That is the formula for conflict.

Although foreign armies have surrounded Jerusalem in the past—even international armies during the crusades—the conflict has always been of a more limited scope. Never before has Jerusalem been a problem for "the world," and never before has there been a fulfillment of Zechariah's prophecy that "all the nations of the earth" would unite to impose their solution. (Zech. 12:3 LB) Now, today, we see such a problem in place, and we see moves afoot in the world community to impose such a solution. Are we also seeing the events Jesus pointed forward to as part of a 'sign' to watch for in the end times? Jesus said:

"When these things begin to take place, stand up and lift up your heads, because your redemption is drawing near . . . it will come upon all those who live on the face of the whole earth."

—Luke 21:28 NIV

Everyone living today has reason to be concerned and to investigate the significance of these events and the prophecies that foretold them.

But the Bible Contradicts Itself—Doesn't It?

'The Bible contradicts itself!' That is probably the most common excuse cited by people who want to ignore what it says about the coming international confrontation over Jerusalem and the end of the world—and to ignore what it says about other matters. But, is that a valid excuse? Does the Bible really contradict itself? At first glance it may appear to.

For example, the New Testament reports that Jesus said that his followers should

"Take nothing for your journey—neither staffs, nor wallet, nor bread, nor money."

—Luke 9:3

And it also reports that he told his followers,

"whoever has a purse, let him take it, and likewise a wallet"

—Luke 22:36

Isn't that a contradiction?

Similarly, the Old Testament prophets say,

". . . they shall beat their swords into plowshares, and their spears into pruninghooks . . ."

—Isaiah 2:4 KJV

But the Old Testament also says,

"Beat your plowshares into swords, and your pruninghooks into spears . . ."

—Joel 3:10 KJV

Isn't that a contradiction, as well?

On the surface, these may appear to be contradictions. And they were worded that way in those passages intentionally by the divine Author who inspired Scripture. Why? Because God inspired the Bible not only to instruct disciples, but also to separate people—to separate those who really want the truth from those who don't care enough to probe deeply:

"For the word of God is alive and active. Sharper than any double-edged sword, it penetrates even to dividing soul and spirit, joints and marrow; it judges the thoughts and attitudes of the heart."

—Hebrews 4:12 NIV

The written word of God separates people, judging the thoughts and attitudes of their hearts, depending on how they respond to the message. Such a separation occurred even among the audiences that heard Jesus speak in person when he walked the earth two thousand years ago. For example, when Jesus spoke on one occasion, even many of his own followers had difficulty accepting what he said:

"When the followers of Jesus heard this, many of them said, 'This teaching is hard. Who can accept it?' . . . After Jesus said this, many of his followers left him and stopped following him."

—John 6:60-66 NCV

But those who sincerely wanted to know God's will would come to Jesus privately after his public speaking, and ask him to explain what he meant:

"Jesus used stories to tell all these things to the people; he always used stories to teach them. . . . Then Jesus left the crowd and went into the house. His followers came to him and said, 'Explain to us the meaning of the story . . .'"

—Matthew 13:34-36 NCV

In a similar way, we should read the Bible prayerfully, asking God to help us understand what we read. And we should wait patiently for that understanding to be given to us.

So, what about the apparent contradictions noted at the beginning of this chapter? Are they really contradictions?

Jesus really did tell the disciples to take "no wallet, no money in their purse" on one occasion, and then later told them, "whoever has a purse, let him take it, and likewise a wallet." (Luke 9:3 and 22:36) But he was *not* contradicting himself; rather, he was giving them different instructions on different occasions under different circumstances—changed circumstances that required a different course of action on their part.

This can be best understood by reading the apparently contradictory statements in their own contexts, where the surrounding verses show what was going on at the time the words were spoken.

On the first occasion, Jesus was sending out the disciples on their first preaching tour apart from him:

"He sent them out to preach the Kingdom of God, and to heal the sick. He said to them, 'Take nothing for your journey—neither staffs, nor wallet, nor bread, nor money; neither have two coats apiece. Into whatever house you enter, stay there, and depart from there. As many as don't receive you, when you depart from that

city, shake off even the dust from your feet for a testimony against them.' They departed, and went throughout the villages, preaching the Good News, and healing everywhere."

The second occasion was at the end of his earthly ministry, when Jesus knew that the disciples would have to carry on after his death, in the midst of hostility and persecution. So, he told them to be ready for trouble—and told them it would be different from when he sent them out earlier:

"He said to them, 'When I sent you out without purse, and wallet, and shoes, did you lack anything?'

"They said, 'Nothing.'

"Then he said to them, 'But now, whoever has a purse, let him take it, and likewise a wallet. Whoever has none, let him sell his cloak, and buy a sword. '"

—Luke 22:35-36

So, when read in their full context, there is no contradiction. Jesus gave his followers one set of instructions for one set of circumstances, and different instructions for dealing with changed circumstances later on. They would not need a wallet or purse when he sent them out to preach during his earthly ministry because they would find receptive audiences who would provide for their needs, but after his death and resurrection Jesus' followers would face persecution, and from then on they would need to carry their own wallet or purse.

It is much the same with other supposed contradictions that enemies of the Bible message point to as an excuse for not listening. They are usually taken out of context. A closer examination of surrounding verses makes it clear that differences are due to different circumstances, different audiences, or different speakers trying to accomplish different goals in different situations. There is nothing contradictory about that.

A closer look at the apparently contradictory Old Testament quotes about swords and plowshares presented at the beginning of this chapter reveals the different circumstances surrounding each passage. Isaiah was speaking of the peace that will prevail in God's coming Kingdom under the Messiah when he wrote that

". . . they shall beat their swords into plowshares, and their spears into pruninghooks . . ."

—Isaiah 2:4 KJV

But the prophet Joel wrote of a time before that peace is established—the fast-approaching time of conflict that we are discussing in this book—a time

15

when all the nations will come against Israel, and when God will wage war against the nations. In preparation for this final battle, God's messenger challenges the nations. He calls the nations to get ready by beating their plowshares into swords:

"'In those days and at that time, when I will make things better for Judah and Jerusalem, I will gather all the nations together and bring them down into the Valley Where the LORD Judges. There I will judge them, because those nations scattered my own people Israel and forced them to live in other nations. They divided up my land and threw lots for my people. . . .'

"Announce this among the nations: Prepare for war! Wake up the soldiers! Let all the men of war come near and attack.

"Make swords from your plows, and make spears from your hooks for trimming trees.

"Let even the weak person say, 'I am a soldier.'

"All of you nations, hurry, and come together in that place.

"LORD, send your soldiers to gather the nations.

"'Wake up, nations, and come to attack in the Valley Where the LORD Judges. There I will sit to judge all the nations on every side.'

"There are huge numbers of people in the Valley of Decision, because the LORD's day of judging is near in the Valley of Decision. . . . The LORD will roar like a lion from Jerusalem; his loud voice will thunder from that city, and the sky and the earth will shake. But the LORD will be a safe place for his people, a strong place of safety for the people of Israel.

"'Then you will know that I, the LORD your God, live on my holy Mount Zion. Jerusalem will be a holy place, and strangers will never even go through it again.'"

—Joel 3:-17 NCV

Other supposed Bible contradictions similarly disappear when examined more closely in their full context.

Many of the Prophecies Have Already Come True

Do you question the reliability of the Bible's prophecies about Israel and the end of the world? Most people are skeptical. The public media surround us with explanations of this world, its history and current events, that completely ignore God and the Bible. Even many clergymen ridicule the Bible and dismiss it as a book filled with myths, fairy tales and contradictions—interesting poetic literature, but not to be taken seriously in much of what it says.

The human writers of Bible knew that people would view their writings this way. The Apostle Peter wrote,

"I want you to think about the words the holy prophets spoke in the past, and remember the command our Lord and Savior gave us through your apostles. It is most important for you to understand what will happen in the last days. People will laugh at you. They will live doing the evil things they want to do. They will say, 'Jesus promised to come again. Where is he? Our fathers have died, but the world continues . . .'"

—2 Peter 3:2-4 NCV

And many people today do, indeed, laugh at anyone who speaks of prophecy being fulfilled and Jesus coming again.

But what is the Bible's actual track record in matters of history and prophecy?

The first thing a reader of the Bible will notice is the honesty and candor of its historical account. While ancient pagan history books typically glorify kings and emperors as godlike heroes without mentioning their flaws and human frailties, the Bible describes in detail, the strengths and the weaknesses of the kings of Israel, the ancient prophets and the apostles of Christ. When telling about great king David, the Old Testament includes not only his victories, but also the sad episodes of his adulterous affair with Bathsheba and his fawning over his rebellious son Absalom. It presents Solomon as the wisest king who ever lived, but also concludes with complete candor that he eventually fell into idolatry when he broke God's laws by marrying foreign wives and then catered to their requests to worship false gods. When the New Testament speaks of Jesus' apostles, it tells how they argued among themselves, how Judas betrayed Jesus, how Peter caved in to peer pressure on more than one occasion, how Thomas doubted Jesus' resurrection, and how Paul and Barnabas were kept from working together by a sharp disagreement. Such honesty and candor inspires confidence.

Unlike ancient myths that are set 'once upon a time' in 'a land far away,' the history recorded in the Bible speaks of specific times, actual places and historical persons—confirmed by contemporary secular histories and by modern archaeology. The Bible relates events in Israel and Judah to specific years in the reigns of Babylonian, Persian and Roman emperors known to secular historians. For example, Zechariah prophesied "In the eighth month, in the second year of Darius," the Medo-Persian emperor. (Zech. 1:1) It was due to a Roman census that Jesus' mother Mary traveled to Bethlehem and gave birth to him there, when "a decree went out from Caesar Augustus that all the world should be enrolled. This was the first enrollment made when Quirinius was governor of Syria." (Luke 2:1-2) John the Baptist began preaching "in the fifteenth year of the reign of Tiberius Caesar, Pontius Pilate being governor of Judea, and Herod being tetrarch of Galilee, and his brother Philip tetrarch of the region of Ituraea and Trachonitis, and Lysanias tetrarch of Abilene." (Luke 3:1)

Of course, honesty, candor and historical accuracy do not by themselves prove the Bible to be God's inspired Word. But prophecy does supply the additional needed proof. Men find it difficult to predict next week's weather. But the Bible contains so many predictions of future events that have come true with such consistent accuracy—even centuries later—that these fulfillments could not possibly have been due to chance. The One who inspired the writers of the Bible must have known and/or controlled the future—something only God could do.

The prophecies that prove the divine inspiration of the Scriptures fall into a number of categories.

Prophecies about the Messiah or Christ

The ancient Hebrew writers of the Old Testament wrote hundreds of years before Christ, but their writings include a number of prophecies that were fulfilled centuries later in the life and ministry of Jesus. "Beginning from Moses and from all the prophets, he explained to them in all the Scriptures the things concerning himself." (Luke 24:27)

For example, Micah 5:2 indicates that the promised Messiah would come from the town of Bethlehem in Judah, and this actually took place when Jesus was born in Bethlehem as recorded at Matthew 2:1-6 and Luke 2:4-7.

Psalm 22, written by king David roughly a thousand years before Christ, begins with words Jesus would speak on the cross (verse 1; compare Matt. 27:46 and Mark 15:34), goes on to describe how they would pierce his hands and his feet (verse 16), how enemies would ridicule him as he hung on the cross (verses 7-8; compare Matt. 27:41-43), and how they would cast lots and divide his clothing (verse 18; compare Matt. 27:35, Mark 15:24, Luke 23:34 and John 19:24).

Other prophecies that Jesus fulfilled centuries later include that he would be born of a virgin, that he would be a descendant of king David, that he would live in Nazareth, that he would preach in Galilee, that he would be betrayed for thirty pieces of silver, and that he would be buried in a rich man's tomb. There are actually dozens of Old Testament prophecies that were fulfilled in Christ. You will encounter them as you read the four Gospels. Or you can find them by searching the Internet.

Prophecies about the God of Abraham

There are prophecies throughout the Old Testament and the New Testament to the effect that the gods of the gentile nations—Baal, Ashtoreth, Chemosh, Dagon, Artemis, Zeus and the rest—would be abandoned and forgotten, while the God of Abraham would come to be worshiped worldwide by people of all nations.

Such predictions may have seemed laughable when they were made, because those other gods were much more popular than the unseen God of the tiny Hebrew nation, but today there are billions Christians, Jews and Muslims in all the nations of the world who profess to worship the God of Abraham.

The Bible's prophecies on this matter were written during an era when each nation had its own gods and goddesses. The Ammonites worshipped Molech, and sacrificed their children as part of that worship. The people of Phoenicia and Canaan bowed down to Baal and Ashtoreth. The nation of Moab served their god Chemosh. The Philistines prostrated themselves before Dagon. The Greeks in Ephesus shouted praise to their goddess Artemis. The Egyptians, Greeks and Romans worshipped their emperors and pharaohs as gods, along with a whole pantheon of pagan deities. But the people of Israel worshipped the unseen Creator of the universe, who revealed himself to Abraham and Abraham's offspring by the name Yahweh or Jehovah—the Hebrew tetragrammaton or word of four letters, YHWH (rendered in most modern English translations as LORD).

How many people today still worship Molech, Chemosh or Dagon? A better question might be, How many people today have even heard of these long-lost 'gods'? How many cities throughout the world can boast of temples where throngs of people assemble to pray to the Greek and Roman deities? But the God of Abraham has people who profess to worship him today in Jewish synagogues, in Catholic, Protestant and Orthodox churches and in Muslim mosques throughout the earth.

Did the God of Abraham win worshipers worldwide because the nations sponsoring other gods ceased to exist? At first glance, that might seem to explain why Molech, Chemosh and Dagon find few faithful adherents today— the nations of Ammon, Phoenicia and Moab are no longer on the map. But, wait! Israel, too, ceased to exist as a nation some two thousand years ago, and wasn't re-established until very recently in 1948. Yet the God of Israel survived and gained worshipers throughout the earth. Moreover, Egypt still exists as a nation, but the gods of the pharaohs are long gone. The vast majority of Egyptians today profess to worship the God of Abraham. Greece and Rome are still on the map, but the Greeks worship the God of Abraham, and Rome has become synonymous with the Roman Catholic faith that elevates the God of Abraham and his Messiah or Christ.

Could it be a mere coincidence, then, that the God of Israel has worshipers everywhere, while the gods of Israel's ancient neighbors have faded into oblivion? No, this is exactly what the Bible prophesied would occur.

The Old Testament was written over a period of hundreds of years in the Hebrew language, and it was completed long before the third century B.C., when it was translated into Greek in Alexandria, Egypt. Contained within that Old Testament, while the pantheon of pagan gods were still actively worshiped, were these ancient prophecies about the God of Abraham:

"All the ends of the world shall remember and turn unto the LORD: and all the kindreds of the nations shall worship before thee."

—Psalm 22:27 KJV

"All the earth shall worship thee, and shall sing unto thee; they shall sing to thy name."

—Psalm 66:4 KJV

"That thy way may be known upon earth, thy saving health among all nations."

—Psalm 67:2 KJV

"God shall bless us; and all the ends of the earth shall fear him."

—Psalm 67:7

"All nations whom thou hast made shall come and worship before thee, O LORD; and shall glorify thy name."

—Psalm 86:9 KJV

"O LORD . . . the Gentiles shall come unto thee from the ends of the earth, and shall say, Surely our fathers have inherited lies, vanity, and things wherein there is no profit. Shall a man make gods unto himself, and they are no gods."

—Jeremiah 16:19-20 KJV

"And it shall come to pass, that every one that is left of all the nations which came against Jerusalem shall even go up from year to year to worship the King, the LORD of hosts."

"'My name will be great among the nations, from the rising to the setting of the sun. In every place incense and pure offerings will be brought to my name, because my name will be great among the nations,' says the LORD Almighty."

—Malachi 1:11 NIV

How unlikely these words would have seemed to non-Israelites at the time when they were written, if non-Israelites would even have bothered to read the religious writings of the Jews!

Hundreds of years later the New Testament was completed and began circulating in multiple copies during the lifetime of those who encountered Jesus in the flesh—at a time when pagan Roman Caesars still ruled the world and compelled people to worship them as gods. Yet these early Christian writings, too, prophesy the same thing about the God of Abraham:

"Who shall not fear thee, O Lord, and glorify thy name? for thou only art holy: for all nations shall come and worship before thee; for thy judgments are made manifest."

—Revelation 15:4 KJV

How unlikely this, too, must have seemed at a time when the powerful Roman empire had only recently crushed Jewish nationalism, tore down the Jewish temple in Jerusalem, scattered the Jewish captives to the four corners of the empire, and was in the process of hunting down and publicly executing the remaining followers of the Jewish Messiah Jesus!

Yet, in spite of overwhelming odds, these ancient biblical prophecies have proved true. Paul, Barnabas and other early Christian disciples traveled far and wide, following Jesus' instructions to "go and make followers of all people in the world" (Matt. 28:19 NCV) and trusting Jesus' assurance that, "you will receive power when the Holy Spirit has come upon you; and you shall be My witnesses both in Jerusalem, and in all Judea and Samaria, and even to the remotest part of the earth." (Acts 1:8 NASB) Wherever they went among the Gentile nations 'ten men' would accept the message about the Jewish Messiah and would take up worshiping the God of the Bible, as foretold centuries earlier by the Hebrew prophet Zechariah: "Thus says Yahweh of Armies: 'In those days, ten men will take hold, out of all the languages of the nations, they will take hold of the skirt of him who is a Jew, saying, "We will go with you, for we have heard that God is with you."'" (Zechariah 8:23) And those who became believers went on to share the Bible's message with others, spreading the message of the God of the Bible far and wide.

The result is that today there are Christians in every land—along with Jews and Muslims who also profess to worship the God of Abraham. Yes, the God of Abraham is worshiped today by people in all the nations of the earth, just as prophesied in the Bible thousands of years ago. Against all odds, these ancient prophecies have come true—a stunning proof that the Bible is God's inspired Word.

Prophecies about Jerusalem, the Jewish people and Israel

As far back as the books of Moses written more than three thousand years ago, the Bible foretold that the Jewish people would be uprooted from the Promised Land and would be scattered throughout the world, hated by people everywhere, only to be restored as a nation thousands of years later, shortly before the end of the world. Impossible as it may have seemed, the Roman empire carried out that worldwide scattering and the British empire later facilitated the regathering.

Through Moses, God brought the nation of Israel into a covenant, a solemn agreement to keep the complete set of laws and commandments He gave them. "These are the words of the covenant which the LORD commanded Moses to make with the sons of Israel." (Deuteronomy 29:1 NASB) If they kept the covenant, they would receive a long string of blessings specifically listed as part of the agreement. But, if they broke the covenant, there would be punishments in store for the nation. The ultimate punishment would be the breakup of the nation and the scattering of the Jewish people to live as strangers in the territories of other nations.

"But it shall come about, if you do not obey the LORD your God . . . the LORD will scatter you among all peoples, from one end of the earth to the other end of the earth."

—Deuteronomy 28:15, 64 NASB

Though the Jewish people would remain in this scattered condition, without a homeland of their own, for a very long, long time, this scattering would not be permanent. They would eventually be returned to the Promised Land:

". . . then the LORD thy God will turn thy captivity, and have compassion upon thee, and will return and gather thee from all the nations, whither the LORD thy God hath scattered thee . . . from thence will he fetch thee: And the LORD thy God will bring thee into the land which thy fathers possessed, and thou shalt possess it."

—Deuteronomy 30:3-5 KJV

". . . the LORD will . . . assemble the dispersed of Israel, and gather together the scattered of Judah from the four corners of the earth."

—Isaiah 11:11-12 Jewish Publication Society of America

There were relatively brief periods of captivity forced on the Jews by the Assyrian empire and later by the Babylonian empire. Much of the population was carried captive to Babylon for about seventy years, with a large number of escapees fleeing in the other direction, to Egypt, around the sixth century B.C. But the real scattering of the Jews to the four corners of the earth was yet future. Jesus, the Jewish Messiah, repeated the prophecy in these words:

"'And they shall fall by the edge of the sword and be led away captive into all nations: and Jerusalem shall be trodden down of the Gentiles, until the times of the Gentiles be fulfilled.'"

—Luke 21:24 KJV

Within the lifetime of those who witnessed Christ's crucifixion, a Jewish uprising against Rome was crushed brutally by the imperial armies. The Romans demolished Jerusalem and its temple and sold the Jews into slavery throughout the empire, scattering them to the four corners of the earth, into all the nations.

Not only were the Jews scattered worldwide, but they were also hated worldwide—just at the Bible prophesied:

"'I will pursue them with the sword, famine and plague and will make them abhorrent to all the kingdoms of the earth and an object of cursing and horror, of scorn and reproach, among all the nations where I drive them.'"

—Jeremiah 29:18 NIV

"You will be a hated thing to the nations where the L ORD sends you: they will laugh at you and make fun of you."

—Deuteronomy 28:37 NCV

Pogroms and anti-Semitism followed the Jewish people wherever they went.

Normally, such worldwide scattering and persecution would have spelled the end of a people and a nation. To all appearances, there would never again be a Jewish state in Palestine. The Romans ruled the ruins of Jerusalem until the empire began to fall apart. Then the eastern empire ruled from Byzantium or Constantinople. With the rise of Islam, Muslims took control. Over the centuries the land changed hands as European Crusaders and the Arab warriors of Islamic Jihad pushed each other back and forth across the war-torn terrain. For hundreds of years—nearly two thousand years, in fact—Gentiles trampled upon Jerusalem. Would the Jewish state ever be restored? Only a miracle could bring that about.

However, that miracle had been promised in Bible prophecy. Although it took two world wars to accomplish it, the miracle occurred as the hand of God pushed world events in that direction, and the prophecy was fulfilled.

World War I was still raging, and the Ottoman Turks still held Jerusalem when, on June 4, 1917, Jules Cambon, Secretary General of the French Foreign Ministry, wrote this in an official letter to Jewish Zionist leader Nahum Sokolow:

> "... it would be a deed of justice and reparation to assist, by the protection of the Allied Powers, in the renaissance of the Jewish nationality in that Land from which the people of Israel were exiled so many centuries ago."

Five months later, on November 2, 1917, British foreign secretary Arthur James Lord Balfour wrote in a letter to a Jewish peer in the House of Lords, an official pronouncement that has since been dubbed the Balfour Declaration:

> "His Majesty's Government view with favour the establishment in Palestine of a national home for the Jewish people . . ."

(Readers familiar with Bible history will find these proclamations reminiscent of the orders issued by rulers of the ancient Medo-Persian empire to rebuild Jerusalem and its temple after the Babylonian exile, as recorded in the Old Testament books of Nehemiah and Ezra.)

When British forces under General Allenby took Jerusalem from the Ottoman Turks in December, 1917, a Jewish Legion of five thousand Jews from many nations formed part of the victorious army. Under a Mandate from the League of Nations, Britain administered the territory. Meanwhile, a steady influx of Jewish immigrants began to arrive.

As though to thwart the fulfillment of prophecy, Hitler's Nazi government arose and began the systematic slaughter of six million Jews in gas chambers and ovens. It took the Second World War to stop this demonic Holocaust and to keep the prophecy on track to fulfillment. But enough Jews survived to see the formation of the State of Israel in 1948. The Bible indeed proved to be a book of true prophecy.

These prophecies, undeniably fulfilled by events thousands of years after they were written, offer indisputable evidence of the truthfulness, inspiration and reliability of the Bible.

Unlike fanciful religious writings and fairy tales, the Bible speaks of the real world and its past and future events. The existence of ancient kings and kingdoms described in Scripture has been verified, time and again, by archaeological discoveries. In fact, archaeologists unearthing the history of the Middle East have long used the Bible as a guide, to help them know what to look for and where to dig for it. Besides its 'end times' prophecies concerning Messiah's return, his coming Kingdom of God, and the end of the corrupt 'world' as we know it, the Bible also contains many prophecies that have already undergone fulfillment. Their accurate fulfillment hundreds or thousands of years later offers convincing evidence to help us put faith in the Bible as the Word of God.

Jerusalem a Problem for the Whole World
—as Foretold

It would be an understatement to remark that political and military control over the city of Jerusalem has changed hands many times over the years. In most cases, however, the city itself was not the main focus of the war or the diplomatic negotiations that resulted in the change of ownership, at least from the standpoint of the generals and the diplomats. Empires were on the move, and Jerusalem just happened to be in the way. It's location at the intersection of lines connecting the continents of Europe, Asia and Africa placed it in the path of many a large-scale conquest.

The exceptions were the numerous Jewish campaigns and revolts, aimed at wresting control away from occupying Gentile powers, and, of course, the Christian Crusades and Islamic Jihads, because these "holy" wars were often targeted specifically at control of Jerusalem.

The Crusades and opposing Jihads which raged from the eleventh through the thirteenth centuries involved the nations of Christendom and those of Islam, but it would be an exaggeration to say that Jerusalem had become a problem for the whole world during that period, or that all the nations of the world had united to impose a solution. Christendom then stretched across Europe, and the Muslim states covered North Africa and the Middle East. Few, if any, inhabitants of China, Japan or sub-Saharan Africa were following those developments, much less actually involved in them, and the Americas (which had not yet received that name) were totally out of the picture. Moreover, the Crusades and Jihads pitted groups of nations against each other for control of Jerusalem; they had not come together to impose an international regime. The time Zechariah predicted when Jerusalem would be a 'stone burdening the whole world' and when 'all the nations would unite' to impose a solution was yet future. (Zechariah 12:2-3)

Today, however, we do indeed see a situation in which Jerusalem has become a problem for the whole world, and in which the nations, already united through the United Nations organization, are debating using that organization to impose a solution. The radical Islamic suicide bombings that were once confined to Israel, with the aim, in part, of restoring Muslim control over Jerusalem, have now spread worldwide. American interests around the globe have become the target of such attacks, and a principal argument of justification offered by the attackers and the groups sponsoring them has been that America supports Israel. United States embassies have been blown up in Africa, a nightclub full of international tourists has been bombed in Bali, Indonesia, and, of course, the twin towers of the World Trade Center in New York City have been destroyed, killing mostly Americans, but with citizens from dozens of countries included among the fatalities.

America responded to the destruction of September 11, 2001, with a "war against terror" that has involved nations around the globe. The United States military targeted Afghanistan, and drove from power the Taliban regime that had hosted and supported Osama Bin Laden and his Al Quaeda training camps. But terrorists were also reported to have held secret meetings in places far from the Middle East to plan the September 11 attacks. The FBI began working with governments to arrest alleged conspirators in Spain, France, England, Italy, Germany, Indonesia, the Philippines and elsewhere. American soldiers entered the Philippines as "advisors" to help hunt down Islamic militants. Jerusalem had become a problem for all of these nations.

Concurrent with all of this, letters laden with deadly anthrax spores threatened American postal workers and shut down major government buildings for decontamination. Unsolved for years, that germ warfare attack was blamed by many on the same terrorist network responsible for the suicide bombings, the terrorists whose complaint revolved around the status of Jerusalem. Copycat hoaxes turned up envelopes with white powder from South America to the Far East and from Europe to Africa. Whether correctly or mistakenly in this case, the struggle for control over Jerusalem was seen by many as being at the center of this uproar.

America and coalition forces next attacked Iraq to depose the regime of Saddam Hussein, whose alleged weapons of mass destruction threatened the United States and its allies, most notably Israel. The Jewish state had sent attack aircraft to destroy an Iraqi nuclear facility in 1982, and one of Saddam's constant propaganda themes had been recruitment of an army of millions of civilians to "march on Jerusalem." Israel had been struck by several Scud missiles fired from Iraq during the Gulf War of 1992, and so was clearly within range and was a prime target. The Iraqi government had also been making cash payments to the families of suicide bombers who died attacking Jews in Israel. Some American critics of the George W. Bush administration blamed the president's push for war on his support for Israel and his determination to save Israel from attack by alleged Iraqi weapons of mass destruction.

Nations throughout the world have been directly involved in all of these events, or at least have participated in the international debate and the political maneuverings relating to Afghanistan, Iraq and the "war on terror." Nations everywhere have been forced to modify procedures relating to air travel, institute improved security measures, and keep track of suspected terrorists or terrorist support organizations within their borders.

The whole world has followed all of these developments on TV and on the Internet, and the whole world has been terrorized. Jerusalem has indeed become a problem for the whole world. Each time there was another suicide bombing in Israel, or another Israeli military incursion into Palestinian areas, the world shuddered and speculated on how the international terrorists would respond. Where would they strike next?

Yes, Jerusalem is now a problem "burdening the whole world." But, are the nations also uniting to impose a solution, as the prophet Zechariah foretold? (Zech. 12:2-3)

Prior to the twentieth century and the formation of the League of Nations in the wake of World War One, it would have been difficult to conceive of all the nations of the world uniting to do anything at all, let alone uniting to mobilize armies against Jerusalem. But, one of the earliest official acts of that League of Nations was to grant the British government a Mandate to rule over Palestine, including Jerusalem.

Prior to the late 1990's and the beginning of the new millennium, it would have been difficult to conceive of the League's successor, the United Nations, considering mobilizing forces against Jerusalem. The prevailing concept had always been that national sovereignty trumped United Nations authority. United Nations peacekeepers generally assisted in conflicts between member nations, with the consent of both parties, but the world body scrupulously avoided interfering in the internal affairs of member states.

In fact, from the time of its founding at the end of the Second World War, the U.N. had been viewed as largely a debating society, when it came to issues of war and peace. As a world government, it had active social service agencies such as UNESCO (United Nations Educational, Scientific and Cultural Organization) and UNICEF (United Nations International Children's Emergency Fund), and it accomplished a lot in the way of promoting world communication and commerce, but it did not have a strong police force.

And it still does not. After all, how can a policeman armed with only a billy club subdue brawlers brandishing knives and guns? Comparatively speaking, that is what peacekeeping forces in white trucks marked "UN" would be up against, if they were to confront an uncooperative nation determined to use its jet fighters, bombers and tanks aggressively. United Nations peacekeepers have never been heavily armed by modern military standards.

The Korean War may come to mind as an exception. The United Nations organization was still in its infancy when, in 1950, the Soviet Union decided to boycott sessions of the Security Council. In the absence of a Soviet veto, the Council invoked military sanctions against North Korea and invited member states to come to the aid of South Korea. American troops then led those from many other nations as "United Nations forces" in a military campaign sanctified as a U.N. mission. These U.N. forces waged full scale war with everything short of nuclear weapons. But that was an unusual circumstance that has not repeated itself. Major powers have learned not to boycott the Security Council's meetings.

Recent decades, however, have seen more and more authority vested in U.N. agencies, together with greater reliance on blue-helmeted U.N. peacekeeping forces. Toward the end of 2002 and during the early months of 2003, the Security Council earnestly debated whether or not to authorize military action to enforce its earlier resolutions about disarming Saddam Hussein's regime in Iraq. In 2011 the Security Council authorized military action in support of the Libyan rebellion against Colonel Muammar Qaddafi, and U.N. forces in Cote d'Ivoire engaged in military assaults against the forces of incumbent President Laurent Gbagbo.

Will such actions prove to be a dress rehearsal for a military move by the United Nations against Israel? Time will tell. But the necessary U.N. resolutions that could lead up to such actions are already in place. If the Security Council could debate the possibility of calling for military action against Iraq to enforce its resolutions, it could certainly do the same with regard to Israel. In fact, some critics of the American push for a resolution authorizing force against Iraq argued that it would be a double standard to take action against Iraq and not against Israel.

Even now, although the world has not yet come together to authorize joint military force against Israel, it has already come together to oppose Israeli control of Jerusalem. It is only the military enforcement that is lacking, as of this writing.

Over the course of many decades, the groundwork has progressively been laid for international intervention to determine Jerusalem's fate.

Following the Allied conquest of the city at the end of 1917, Britain ruled Jerusalem and all of the land of Israel under a Mandate issued by the League of Nations, predecessor of the United Nations. This did not appear, at that time, to be hostile to Jewish interests concerning the city. Prior to that, Jerusalem had been in the hands of the Ottoman Turks—Muslims who had no intention of establishing Jewish sovereignty. But the British government had, by its Balfour Declaration of 1917, announced that "His Majesty's Government view with favour the establishment in Palestine of a national home for the Jewish people, and will use their best endeavours to facilitate the achievement of this object." So, the League's grant of a Mandate for Britain to rule the area appeared to be a pro-Jewish move. Still, it established a precedent for international determination of Jerusalem's fate by a world body.

In 1947, after the League's demise, a United Nations resolution recommended partitioning the mandated territory of Palestine into two independent nations, one Jewish and the other Arab, and, after British forces withdrew, the nations of Israel and Jordan were born the following year. Thus, the United Nations has been involved with the modern state of Israel since before its birth.

United Nations General Assembly Resolution 181 called for the partition of the British-ruled Palestine Mandate into a Jewish state and an Arab state. It was approved on November 29, 1947, and included the following provisions relating to Jerusalem:

I.A.3. Independent Arab and Jewish States and the Special International Regime for the City of Jerusalem, set forth in Part III of this Plan, shall come into existence in Palestine two months after the evacuation of the armed forces of the mandatory Power has been completed but in any case not later than 1 October 1948. The boundaries of the Arab State, the Jewish State, and the City of Jerusalem shall be as described in Parts II and III below.
. . .

C. THE CITY OF JERUSALEM

The boundaries of the City of Jerusalem are as defined in the recommendations on the City of Jerusalem. (See Part III, section B, below).

. . .

Part III. - City of Jerusalem

A. SPECIAL REGIME

The City of Jerusalem shall be established as a corpus separatum under a special international regime and shall be administered by the United Nations. The Trusteeship Council shall be designated to discharge the responsibilities of the Administering Authority on behalf of the United Nations.

B. BOUNDARIES OF THE CITY

The City of Jerusalem shall include the present municipality of Jerusalem plus the surrounding villages and towns, the most eastern of which shall be Abu Dis; the most southern, Bethlehem; the most western, 'Ein Karim (including also the built-up area of Motsa); and the most northern Shu'fat, as indicated on the attached sketch-map (annex B).

C. STATUTE OF THE CITY

The Trusteeship Council shall, within five months of the approval of the present plan, elaborate and approve a detailed statute of the City which shall contain, inter alia, the substance of the following provisions:

1. Government machinery; special objectives. The Administering Authority in discharging its administrative obligations shall pursue the following special objectives:

i. To protect and to preserve the unique spiritual and religious interests located in the city of the three great monotheistic faiths throughout the world, Christian, Jewish and Moslem; to this end to ensure that order and peace, and especially religious peace, reign in Jerusalem;

ii. To foster cooperation among all the inhabitants of the city in their own interests as well as in order to encourage and support the peaceful development of the mutual relations between the two Palestinian peoples throughout the Holy Land; to promote the security, well-being and any constructive measures of development of the residents having regard to the special circumstances and customs of the various peoples and communities.

2. Governor and Administrative staff. A Governor of the City of Jerusalem shall be appointed by the Trusteeship Council and shall be responsible to it. He shall be selected on the basis of special qualifications and without regard to nationality. He shall not, however, be a citizen of either State in Palestine.

The Governor shall represent the United Nations in the City and shall exercise on their behalf all powers of administration, including the conduct of external affairs. He shall be assisted by an administrative staff classed as international officers in the meaning of Article 100 of the Charter and chosen whenever practicable from the residents of the city and of the rest of Palestine on a non-discriminatory basis. A detailed plan for the organization of the administration of the city shall be submitted by the Governor to the Trusteeship Council and duly approved by it.

The partition of the territory covered by the British Palestine Mandate resulted in formation of the Jewish state of Israel and the Arab state of Jordan, but the internationalization of Jerusalem specified in General Assembly Resolution 181 failed to occur. Nor did any "Governor of the City of Jerusalem" representing the United Nations ever take office to run the city, as that Resolution required.

However, the United Nations organization has continued to generate new resolutions concerning Jerusalem, with the number of these resolutions now in the hundreds—the vast majority of them condemning the actions of the Jewish state.

These resolutions, often referencing earlier resolutions, continued to protest Israeli control of the city. For example, in 1980 the U.N. Security Council's Resolution 476 declared that the body was

"Reaffirming its resolutions relevant to the character and status of the Holy City of Jerusalem, in particular resolutions 252 (1968),267 (1969), 271 (1969), 298 (1971) and 465 (1980).

. . .

1. Reaffirms the overriding necessity for ending the prolonged occupation of Arab territories occupied by Israel since 1967, including Jerusalem.;

. . .

4. Reiterates that all such measures which have altered the geographic, demographic and historical character and status of the Holy City of Jerusalem are null and void and must be rescinded in compliance with the relevant resolutions of the Security Council.

Consider also the full text of the 1980 U.N. Security Council Resolution 478, which, like Resolution 476, was presented in response to Israeli laws affirming the status of Jerusalem as Israel's capital:

Resolution 478 (1980)

of 20 August 1980

The Security Council,

Recalling its resolution 476 (1980),

Reaffirming again that the acquisition of territory by force is inadmissible,

Deeply concerned over the enactment of a "basic law" in the Israeli Knesset proclaiming a change in the character and status of the Holy City of Jerusalem, with its implications for peace and security.

Noting that Israel has not complied with resolution 476 (1980),

Reaffirming its determination to examine practical ways and means, in accordance with the relevant provisions of the Charter of the United Nations, to secure the full implementation of its resolution 476 (1980), in the event of non-compliance by Israel,

1. Censures in the strongest terms the enactment by Israel of the "basic law" on Jerusalem and the refusal to comply with relevant Security Council resolutions;

2. Affirms that the enactment of the "basic law" by Israel constitutes a violation of international law and does not affect the continued application of the Geneva Convention relative to the Protection of Civilian Persons in Time of War, of 12 August 1949, in the Palestinian and other Arab territories occupied since June 1967, including Jerusalem;

3. Determines that all legislative and administrative measures and actions taken by Israel, the occupying Power, which have altered or purport to alter the character and status of the Holy City of Jerusalem, and in particular the recent "basic law" on Jerusalem, are null and void and must be rescinded forthwith;

4. Affirms also that this action constitutes a serious obstruction to achieving a comprehensive, just and lasting peace in the Middle East;

5. Decides not to recognize the "basic law" and such other actions by Israel that, as a result of this law, seek to alter the character and status of Jerusalem and calls upon:

(a) All Member States to accept this decision;

(b) Those States that have established diplomatic missions at Jerusalem to withdraw such missions from the Holy City

6. Requests the Secretary-General to report to the Security Council on the implementation of the present resolution before 15 November 1980;

7. Decides to remain seized of this serious situation.

Adopted at the 2245th meeting by 14 votes to none, with 1 abstention (United States of America).

And as recently as November 2011, the General Assembly of the United Nations again refers back to and upholds its 1947 resolution on the partition of Palestine, "in particular its provisions regarding the City of Jerusalem":

66/18. Jerusalem

The General Assembly,

Recalling its resolution 181 (II) of 29 November 1947, in particular its provisions regarding the City of Jerusalem,

Recalling also its resolution 36/120 E of 10 December 1981 and all its subsequent relevant resolutions, including resolution 56/31 of 3 December 2001, in which it, inter alia, determined that all legislative and administrative measures and actions taken by Israel, the occupying Power, which have altered or purported to alter the character and status of the Holy City of Jerusalem, in particular the so-called "Basic Law" on Jerusalem and the proclamation of Jerusalem as the capital of Israel, were null and void and must be rescinded forthwith,

Recalling further the Security Council resolutions relevant to Jerusalem, including resolution 478 (1980) of 20 August 1980, in which the Council, inter alia, decided not to recognize the "Basic Law" on Jerusalem,

. . .

```
1. Reiterates its determination that any actions taken by
Israel, the occupying Power, to impose its laws,
jurisdiction and administration on the Holy City of
Jerusalem are illegal and therefore null and void and have
no validity whatsoever, and calls upon Israel to
immediately cease all such illegal and unilateral
measures;

. . .

69th plenary meeting

30 November 2011
```

So, the United Nations still holds the position that Jerusalem should not be part of the state of Israel or under its control—even though Israel views Jerusalem as its capital.

You can read all of the Security Council resolutions concerning Jerusalem by browsing to the United Nations website at www.UN.org. Just follow the links for U.N. bodies, and select "Security Council" and then "Resolutions." Or, to go directly to the resolutions regarding Israel and Palestine, use this direct link valid as of this writing: http://domino.un.org/UNISPAL.NSF/ The resulting page states that there are "over 30,000 text documents" in the collection, so it is necessary to click on document "Type" and then scroll down to "Resolutions" to find a complete list of the hundreds of General Assembly and Security Council resolutions.

These resolutions show that the world organization has not forgotten about the 1947 resolution calling for internationalization of Jerusalem under a governor appointed by the U.N. Most people may have forgotten, but the leaders of the world's nations remember. For example, toward the end of the year 2000 the U.N. General Assembly passed Resolution 57/111 on Jerusalem, in which it specifically references "resolution 181 (II) of 29 November 1947, in particular its provisions regarding the City of Jerusalem," and states, "the international community, through the United Nations, has a legitimate interest in the question of the City of Jerusalem" and that "any actions taken by Israel to impose its laws, jurisdiction and administration on the Holy City of Jerusalem are illegal and therefore null and void and have no validity whatsoever."

It is these resolutions that the world community may eventually seek to enforce through a military confrontation between Israel and all the nations of the world. As noted earlier in this book, British Foreign Secretary Jack Straw said, "the West has been guilty of double standards—on the one hand saying the UN Security Council resolutions on Iraq must be implemented, on the other hand, sometimes appearing rather quixotic over the implementation of resolutions about Israel and Palestine." (From a March 26, 2003 *Jerusalem Post* article titled, "Foreign Ministry slams British PM's linkage of Iraq, Intifada," by Douglas Davis) The U.N. resolutions on Iraq were enforced militarily, so why not the resolutions on Jerusalem?

It is hard to imagine United Nations forces assembling in the region outside Israel and then marching into the country. In half a dozen wars Israel was able to push back the combined armies of all its Arab neighbors. In the 1967 war the Arab armies managed to push ahead twenty miles inside Israel, but then Israel stopped them and pushed them back. Would U.N. forces meet with greater success than the Arabs? Even from a purely secular and strategic standpoint, without giving thought to divine intervention, the task would give pause to any general or military commander.

Moreover, today it is generally known or widely believed that Israel possesses nuclear weapons, although the Jews have never publicly declared themselves a nuclear power. With atomic weapons on both sides, the United States and the Soviet Union faced off for decades without either side daring to stage an all-out attack. A would-be attacker of Israel faces a similar deterrent.

So, how could a situation arise that would actually bring the forces of the United Nations into conflict with Israel over Jerusalem?

We will have to wait to see what happens, of course. But, dramatic changes and reversals have occurred before in global politics. And suicidal military ventures are not unknown in human history.

Yet, it is more common for military powers to back themselves into a corner, where they find themselves forced to act. For example, it would not be difficult to conceive of United Nations peacekeeping forces being invited into Jerusalem's border areas in relatively small numbers as part of an Israeli-Palestinian peace agreement. They might be welcomed by both sides under certain conditions, perhaps as unarmed monitors to report on compliance with agreements, or as lightly armed border guards to secure agreed-upon boundaries. Then, once they were in place, it would not be difficult to imagine the situation deteriorating some time later, and the government of Israel taking a position contrary to what the United Nations felt obligated to enforce. A confrontation between Israeli troops and reinforced U.N. forces could escalate unexpectedly.

Actually, United Nations forces have already been invited into the area; not into Jerusalem, but into the border area of southern Lebanon. Israel welcomed them after its withdrawal in the year 2000 from Lebanese land that had been occupied as an Israeli "security zone" for more than two decades. In July, 2000, the U.N. deployed its first peacekeeping units along the "line of withdrawal," also known as the "blue line," between Israel and Lebanon. Referred to as the United Nations Interim Force, battalions of nearly two hundred soldiers in blue helmets took up positions—armed men and women from Ireland, Ghana, Finland, Fiji, Nepal and India. So, a similar deployment around Jerusalem is not unthinkable.

In fact, numerous proposals have been made, calling for interposing U.N. peacekeepers between the Israelis and the Palestinians, either ahead of a peace agreement or as a means of implementing such an agreement. So far, Israel has refused to allow entry to such international forces, and the United States has blocked efforts in the U.N. Security Council to move in that direction.

But, the political situation can change a rapidly. Nothing illustrates that better than the changes in the United States policy toward Israel under President George W. Bush.

For decades prior to his administration the American policy had been one of official neutrality between Israel and the Palestinians. President Jimmy Carter dealt even handedly with both sides and brought them to the peace table at Camp David. Ronald Reagan pursued the same course during his eight-year administration. And George H. W. Bush (the father of George W. Bush) did likewise. The Bill Clinton White House followed the same policy and brought the Israelis and the Palestinians to the point of a peace agreement that was to have put a Palestinian state in place as early as 1999. Then the status of Jerusalem came up, and negotiations fell apart.

The policy of the new administration of George W. Bush appeared, at first, to be characterized by a lack of interest in the Middle East, altogether. Then, it became clear that, by adopting a hands-off policy, the new president had caused the United States government to change its course with regard to the Israeli-Palestinian conflict. Instead of acting as a neutral power trying to bring both sides to the negotiating table, the United States actually backed the Israeli side. Without strong American pressure to act as a restraint, the government of Israel had the upper hand in dealing with the Palestinians. And with the tacit approval of Washington Israel used to its military superiority to impose a *de facto* solution without further negotiation with the Palestinians. Citing security concerns, Israeli forces simply re-occupied territory previously turned over to the Palestinian Authority.

But, then came September 11, 2001. When Islamic terrorist attacks hit the Pentagon and the World Trade Center, it became clear that Israel's strangulation of Palestinian aspirations in the occupied territories would not settle the matter. Like a balloon that is squeezed in one place, only to expand everywhere else, the violence spread worldwide. As a result, American policy changed course again. Instead of total disengagement, the U.S. became fully engaged, once more, in the Middle East peace process, this time by joining Russia, the European Union and the United Nations to form a Quartet sponsoring an international roadmap for peace.

Similar rapid changes in circumstances and policies could turn a voluntary peacekeeping operation around Jerusalem into a hostile military occupation by blue helmeted United Nations peacekeeping forces. The international attack on Jerusalem long foretold in the Bible could develop from a botched peacekeeping effort. Peacekeepers brought in voluntarily by Israel could turn into the advance guard of an invading army. And a new administration in

Washington could turn Israel's only ally into a neutral observer, or even an opponent.

Am I writing this book to declare to the world that this is what will happen? No. We cannot be certain, at this time, just how the prophecies of an international attack on Jerusalem will see fulfillment.

But we can be certain that Jerusalem has already now become a problem for the whole world, and that the legal framework has already been put in place for the United Nations to oppose Israeli control over the city. In the light of Bible prophecy, this gives us reason to expect the rest of what the Bible predicts to take place in the near future.

Ezekiel's Prophecy: a Coalition Attack on a Restored Israel

Around 2500 years ago the prophet Ezekiel spoke of a time in the distant future when the Jews would return to the land of Israel, the nation would be restored, and then a broad coalition of many nations would attack:

"The LORD spoke his word to me, saying, 'Human, look toward Gog of the land of Magog, the chief ruler of the nations of Meshech and Tubal. Prophesy against him and say, "The LORD God says this: I am against you, Gog, chief ruler of Meshech and Tubal. I will turn you around and put hooks in your jaws. And I will bring you out with all your army, horses, and horsemen, all of whom will be dressed in beautiful uniforms. They will be a large army . . . Persia, Cush, and Put will be with them . . . There will also be Gomer with all its troops and the nation of Togarmah from the far north with all its troops—many nations . . .**

""""After a long time you will be called for service. After those years you will come into a land that has been rebuilt from war. The people in the land will have been gathered from many nations to the mountains of Israel, which were empty for a long time. These people were brought out from the nations . . .

""""You, all your troops, and the many nations with you . . . Now that my people Israel are living in safety, you will know about it. You will come with many people from your place in the far north. You will have a large group with you, a mighty army . . .""""

—Ezekiel 38:1-15 NCV

Some commentators in the past have viewed this passage as foretelling events surrounding Antiochus IV Epiphanes who ruled the Seleucid Empire from 175 BC until his death in 164 BC., and who occupied the land of Israel and tried to force the Jews to give up their laws and customs. Many modern commentators interpret the passage as foretelling a future attack against Israel by Russia and a broad coalition of nations under Russia's leadership seven years before the coming battle of Armageddon.

Throughout the years of the Cold War it was the Soviet Union (primarily Russia) that took the lead in attacking Israel in the United Nations, along with the Arab states. Huge majorities passed countless General Assembly resolutions condemning the Jewish state. Why didn't the U.N. take military action against Israel on the scale of the Korean conflict? America's veto in the Security Council precluded such an attack.

However, the nations surrounding the restored modern state of Israel—its immediate neighbors—did attack more than once over the years. In 1948, after Israel declared its independence, it was invaded by the combined armies of Egypt, Syria, Transjordan (later Jordan), Lebanon, Iraq and Saudi Arabia. Local Palestinian Arab forces also fought the Jews. In 1967 the forces of Egypt, Jordan, Syria and Iraq massed on Israel's borders in obvious preparation for a massive attack, but Israel struck first preemptively in what came to be called the Six Day War. In the War of Attrition (1969-70) Israel's neighbors precipitated frequent clashes along the borders and the 1967 cease-fire lines, with additional guerilla action inside Israel itself. In the Yom Kippur War (or Ramadan War from the Arab perspective) of 1973, the forces of Egypt, Syria and Iraq again attacked the Jewish state.

Although initially backing Israel during the 1948 war and the truce that followed, the early 1950s saw the Soviet Union switch to supporting the Arab states. Russia played a major role in the later multi-national attacks against Israel.

The Russians reportedly supplied much of the sophisticated military equipment used by the Arab side in the 1967 Six Day War. In the 1969-1970 War of Attrition, the Soviet Union participated actively in Egypt's air defense by providing military hardware and thousands of "advisors." According to information supplied by the Israel Defense Forces and published in the Jewish Virtual Library, Russians actually piloted Mig fighter planes, operated the sophisticated radar installations, and launched surface-to-air missiles against Israeli planes. The IAF reported shooting down five Russian pilots. (http://www.jewishvirtuallibrary.org/jsource/Society_&_Culture/69iaf.html)

But the popular identification of Magog and Meshech with Russia and Moscow is the subject of much speculation and debate. Actually, Persia is the only nation in Ezekiel's list that we can identify with certainty; it is the age-old name of the country we call Iran today. Genesis, chapter 10, lists Cush and Put as grandsons of Noah through his son Ham, and Magog, Gomer, Meshech and Tubal as grandsons of Noah through his son Japheth—plus Togarmah as a great-grandson—noting concerning their descendants that "All the families grew and became different nations, each nation with its own land and its own language." (Genesis 10:5 NCV) Commentaries locate these nations across portions of Europe, Asia and Africa.

Ezekiel said these nations would unite to attack a restored state of Israel in the distant future, a land "whose people were gathered from many nations to the mountains of Israel, which had long been desolate." (38:8 NIV) This description could certainly fit the modern state of Israel, populated by Jews who returned to the Promised Land from Europe and the Americas, as well as from Russia.

The attackers would include Iran (Persia) and "many" other nations. The Apostle John's Apocalypse uses similar language to refer to *all* the nations— "the nations in the four corners of the earth—Gog and Magog." (Revelation 20:8) So, Ezekiel's list of nations could likewise represent the entire world community of nations.

There is also a similarity of language between Ezekiel 39 and Revelation 19, which may imply that Ezekiel was writing concerning the same final war discussed in the nineteenth chapter of Revelation. In both passages all the birds are invited to eat the flesh of the world's rulers and their armies, after the nations are defeated by God's forces.

"'. . . Speak to every kind of bird and wild animal: "Come together, come! Come together from all around to my sacrifice, a great sacrifice which I will prepare for you on the mountains of Israel. Eat flesh and drink blood! You are to eat the flesh of the mighty and drink the blood of the rulers of the earth . . . At my table you are to eat until you are full of horses and riders, mighty men and all kinds of soldiers,"' says the LORD God. "'I will show my glory among the nations. All the nations will see my power when I punish them.'"

—Ezekiel 39:17-21 NCV

"Then I saw an angel standing in the sun, and he called with a loud voice to all the birds flying in the sky: 'Come and gather together for the great feast of God so that you can eat the bodies of kings, generals, mighty people, horses and their riders, and the bodies of all people—free, slave, small, and great.' Then I saw the beast and the kings of the earth. Their armies were gathered together to make war against the rider on the horse and his army."

—Revelation 19:17-19 NCV

The Apostle John, who wrote the Revelation under divine inspiration, was familiar with Ezekiel's earlier writings, so his use of similar language would not be a mere accident. Did he mean to imply that he was writing of the same conflict that Ezekiel foretold?

Was Gog's attack in Ezekiel a portrayal of Russia waging war against Israel by proxy through all of its Arab neighbors? Could it be that Ezekiel's prophecy was fulfilled in Russia's mobilizing the United Nations—all the nations of the world—to condemn Israel? Russia and its Arab allies were behind countless General Assembly resolutions and Security Council resolutions condemning the actions of the Jewish state. Or did the prophet write of a future full-scale military attack on Israel by Russia and a limited group of allies? Or was Ezekiel speaking of a move against Israel by all the nations of the world, a final attack that triggers God's wrath at Armageddon?

Time will tell. Bible readers will be in a better position to identify the correct interpretation as the fulfillment of end times prophecy continues to play out.

Will You Have Seven More Years to Decide?

Readers of the popular *Left Behind* fiction series by Tim LaHaye and Jerry Jenkins may feel that they can safely wait and see before choosing to follow Jesus. If Christ returns and they miss the Rapture of the Church to heaven, they can just wait for the second bus.

That second chance after the Rapture is one of the basic teachings of the *Left Behind* novels. According to the story line, a broad coalition of nations led by Russia and Iran stage an all-out attack on Israel (in fulfillment of the prophecies of Ezekiel chapters 38 and 39), that attack is blocked by the invisible hand of divine intervention, and then millions of Christians worldwide are raptured to heaven—followed by a seven-year-long Tribulation, with the final war of Armageddon climaxing the end of the seven years. The characters in the novels who never gave a second thought to the Bible and its prophecies find they have a second chance to do so during the Tribulation. So the story goes.

That view of coming events was popularized by the sale of well over 80 million books, videos and other products in the Left Behind series.

According to the Left Behind books the seven-year Tribulation period will afford seven more years of opportunity to come onto God's side. Jesus returns at the beginning of the seven years, according to that view, and takes his true followers to heaven with him. Then he returns again at the end of the seven years to execute judgment on the rest of mankind.

But that is not the traditional view long held by Bible believing Christians down through the centuries. The Scripture passages Tim LaHaye uses to support his view were all understood quite differently by the great Reformation teachers Martin Luther and John Calvin. Others who agreed with Calvin and Luther rather than the authors of *Left Behind* included William Tyndale (English Bible translator), Jonathan Edwards (Congregationalist missionary in colonial America), Roger Williams (the first Baptist pastor in America), John Knox (early Scottish Presbyterian), John Wesley (Methodist founding father), John Huss (martyred by the Inquisition) and John Wycliffe (Bible translator). None of these Bible scholars saw a seven-year post-rapture Tribulation in Scripture.

The passage where supporters of the Left Behind teaching find their seven years is this:

"Seventy weeks are determined upon thy people and upon thy holy city, to finish the transgression, and to make an end of sins, and to make reconciliation for iniquity, and to bring in everlasting righteousness, and to seal up the vision and prophecy, and to

anoint the most Holy. Know therefore and understand, that from the going forth of the commandment to restore and to build Jerusalem unto the Messiah the Prince shall be seven weeks, and threescore and two weeks: the street shall be built again, and the wall, even in troublous times. And after threescore and two weeks shall Messiah be cut off, but not for himself: and the people of the prince that shall come shall destroy the city and the sanctuary; and the end thereof shall be with a flood, and unto the end of the war desolations are determined. And he shall confirm the covenant with many for one week: and in the midst of the week he shall cause the sacrifice and the oblation to cease, and for the overspreading of abominations he shall make it desolate, even until the consummation, and that determined shall be poured upon the desolate."

—Daniel 9:24-27 KJV

The *New International Version* renders the same verses this way, with that translation's footnotes shown here in parentheses to provide alternative renderings:

"Seventy 'sevens' (Or *'weeks'*; also in verses 25 and 26) are decreed for your people and your holy city to finish (Or *restrain*) transgression, to put an end to sin, to atone for wickedness, to bring in everlasting righteousness, to seal up vision and prophecy and to anoint the most holy. (Or *Most Holy Place*; or *most holy One*) Know and understand this: From the issuing of the decree (Or *word*) to restore and rebuild Jerusalem until the Anointed One (Or *an anointed one*; also in verse 26), the ruler, comes, there will be seven 'sevens,' and sixty-two 'sevens.' It will be rebuilt with streets and a trench, but in times of trouble. After the sixty-two 'sevens,' the Anointed One will be cut off and will have nothing. (Or *off and will have no one*; or *off, but not for himself*) The people of the ruler who will come will destroy the city and the sanctuary. The end will come like a flood: War will continue until the end, and desolations have been decreed. He will confirm a covenant with many for one 'seven.' (Or *'week'*) In the middle of the 'seven' (Or *'week'*) he will put an end to sacrifice and offering. And on a wing *of the temple* he will set up an abomination that causes desolation, until the end that is decreed is poured out on him (Or *it*)." (Or *And one who causes desolation will come upon the pinnacle of the abominable* temple, *until the end that is*

decreed is poured out on the desolated city)" (NIV, Revised Edition of 1983)

So, as you can see from the many alternative readings, this is one of the most obscure passages in the Bible. Many different interpretations are possible.

Although the writers of *Left Behind* claim that Daniel 9:24-27 points to a future seven-year tribulation, the great Bible scholars of the Reformation understood it quite differently. Both Martin Luther and John Calvin apply the seven years to the time of Christ. The final "week" or seven-year period covered Jesus' three-and-a-half year earthly ministry, followed by the work of the Apostles for three and a half years preaching almost exclusively to God's covenant people, the Jews. Christ's sacrificial death at the midpoint of that seven-year "week" caused the animal sacrifices that were offered at Jerusalem's temple to cease having any value in God's eyes.

The portion of this passage that Luther, Calvin and other Reformers understood as applying to Christ, the *Left Behind* authors now apply to the Antichrist instead—a complete reversal of what Bible readers believed for hundreds of years.

LaHaye, Jerry Jenkins and others who share their viewpoint believe that the events they portrayed in the *Left Behind* novels actually "will happen someday." They wrote the books, not to entertain readers, but to present "the truth of end times prophecy in fiction form." (*Kingdom Come: The Final Victory*, pages 355-356) However, their presentation departs from the understanding Bible readers have held for centuries and contradicts Christ's teaching.

Jesus never taught that unbelievers would be 'left behind' for a seven-year-long 'second chance' when he returns. Rather, he said that his coming will be like the days of Noah when eight people entered the safety of the Ark and the wicked world was swept away, and like the days of Lot when that righteous man's family was led to safety while the cities of Sodom and Gomorrah were burnt up. Jesus' parables—the wheat and the tares, the sheep and the goats, the ten talents, the wise and foolish virgins—and his plain teaching make it clear that we must "keep watch, because you do not know on what day your Lord will come." (Matt. 24:42 NIV) His coming will be as it was in the days of Noah and in the days of Lot.

The *Left Behind* novels tell a different story. They show half-hearted occasional churchgoers left behind with a second chance—seven more years to make up their minds about Christ. This teaching is not biblical.

Moreover, as noted above, the 'left behind' scenario was unknown among Bible-believers down through the centuries. Tyndale, Huss, Wycliffe, Knox, Calvin, Luther, Wesley and Charles Haddon Spurgeon were serious students of the Word of God, but they never encountered in Scripture a two-stage return of Christ that would give unbelievers a seven-year reprieve. The founders of the Baptist, Presbyterian, Calvinist, Congregationalist, Lutheran and Reformed traditions would not recognize the beliefs that millions of their nominal adherents today have learned from the popular novels by LaHaye and Jenkins.

By the same token today's churchgoers are largely ignorant of the traditional Protestant understanding of end times prophecy. Hence they are oblivious to the warnings that all the great preachers of the past gave concerning the apostasy, the man of sin, and the antichrist that arose from the ruins of the Roman Empire—entities that continue to lead much of the world's population away from Christ. These enemies of God are seldom named from pulpits today, but they were clearly identified by the great preachers of the Reformation.

During the late 1800's and early 1900's the new teachings of one John Nelson Darby were quietly adopted by one theology professor and then another, by one seminary and then another, by one church and then another, by one denomination and then another. Darby's "dispensationalist" teachings taught his followers to put off the end times prophecies until a supposed future Tribulation. It was more 'politically correct' to accept Islam and the papacy as acceptable alternative viewpoints, and to discard the embarrassing accusations that filled the writings of the Reformation. Now that a few more generations have passed, the teaching of the Reformers has been so completely forgotten that it is foreign to the thinking of most church-goers.

If the *Left Behind* scenario is wrong, does that mean the excitement about end times prophecy that the novels stimulated is also wrong? Far from it! Rather, there is every reason to believe that our Redeemer's coming is imminent. The history of divine intervention in ages past identifies the types of situations that provoke God to act. The flood of Noah's day was sent to cleanse a planet that had become full of sexual immorality and violence, much like today's world. Surely this age of internet pornography, motion picture sex goddesses, and weapons of mass destruction tries the Creator's patience to its limits. If God sent fire and brimstone to destroy Sodom and Gomorrah, when the homosexual practices of those towns brought an outcry to his ears, how much longer will he put up with the open gay pride movement that is spreading like wildfire today, and the world that welcomes it with hardly a cry of complaint? When the builders of the Tower of Babel abandoned God to create an urban society capable of accomplishing the impossible, He stopped them in their tracks. So, what about today's predominantly urban world that boasts of human achievement and looks to science to solve all man's problems? How much farther will God let this world go in crediting blind evolution for the Creator's handiwork, developing nuclear weapons, manipulating the genome, and performing sex-change operations? The One who put a stop to Babel, to Sodom and to the pre-Flood world will soon put a stop to today's antichristian culture—this time through the promised return of his Son.

The failings of *Left Behind* do not in any way negate the scriptural injunctions to "keep watch" and "look forward to the day of God." (Matt. 25:13; 2 Pet.

3:12 NIV) Without *Left Behind*'s promise of a post-Rapture 'second chance,' that biblical warning is to be taken even more seriously.

The seven-year struggle of the *Left Behind* characters against the novels' Antichrist is fast-moving, and therefore captivates modern audiences accustomed to such dramatic action on television and at the movies. But, what about the centuries-long struggle of real-world Christians against the dark forces Martin Luther and John Calvin identified as the real Antichrist? That true story may not be as fast moving, but we should recall that "with the Lord a day is like a thousand years, and a thousand years are like a day." (2 Pet. 3:8 NIV) In fact, the real-life history of this struggle is even more fascinating than the *Left Behind* novels. Take the time to read about how John Huss was burned at the stake for preaching the truth. Read how William Tyndale was killed for translating the Bible and standing up to the Antichrist. Read about modern-day Muslim men and women who learn the Gospel message and embrace Jesus Christ as their Savior and Lord, only to be jailed, abused, stoned or beheaded for the crime of converting to Christianity in strict Islamic nations today.

Unfortunately, the *Left Behind* novels have validated unbelievers' "wait and see" attitude by assuring them of seven more years to get right with God after Christ returns. While the novelists urge their readers to accept Christ *now* rather than later, they undermine this by offering a future tribulation period as a seven-year safety net. If the penalty for postponing a personal decision about Christ is nothing worse than a seven-year adventure after his return, why worry?

However, if the traditional understanding of the Second Coming turns out to be correct, and Christ raptures the Church at the same time that he metes out swift punishment to the rest of the world, the undecided who relied on *Left Behind*'s interpretation may be in for an unpleasant surprise with eternal consequences.

But this is not the place to refute the *Left Behind* teachings point by point. I offer such a refutation in my book *LEFT BEHIND Answered Verse by Verse*, which is available in print, and which can also be read for free online at http://www.LeftBehindAnswered.com.

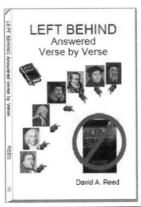

God Doesn't Send Natural Disasters
—Or Does He?

When some prominent preacher declares an earthquake or a devastating storm to be a punishment sent by God, the news media heap ridicule on such a thought. Since "God is love," he doesn't do such things—Or does he?

Even those who don't read the Bible should be familiar with the story of the Jewish people's exodus from Egypt—it has been the topic of epic motion pictures as well as animated features—and the plagues that God sent on Egypt before Pharaoh was finally willing to let Moses' people go. Some of those plagues consisted of destructive pests (frogs, gnats, flies, locusts). Some consisted of diseases afflicting farm animals and diseases afflicting humans. And one of the most devastating plagues was a severe hail storm:

"When Moses raised his walking stick toward the sky, the LORD sent thunder and hail, and lightning flashed down to the earth. So he caused hail to fall upon the land of Egypt. There was hail, and lightning flashed as it hailed—the worst hailstorm in Egypt since it had become a nation. The hail destroyed all the people and animals that were in the fields in all the land of Egypt. It also destroyed everything that grew in the fields and broke all the trees in the fields."

—Exodus 9:23-25 NCV

After they were freed from their slavery in Egypt, God told the people through Moses that they would be blessed if they obeyed his laws, but that they would be punished with disasters if they disobeyed:

"But if you do not obey the LORD your God and carefully follow all his commands and laws I am giving you today, all these curses will come upon you and stay . . . The LORD will punish you with disease, fever, swelling, heat, lack of rain, plant diseases, and mildew until you die. . . . You will plant much seed in your field, but your harvest will be small, because locusts will eat the crop. You will plant vineyards and work hard in them, but you will not pick the grapes or drink the wine, because the worms will eat them."

—Deuteronomy 28:15-22, 38-39 NCV

Over the centuries that followed, the Jewish people actually did rebel against God many times, and he disciplined them many times by sending troubles upon them, including wars, famines and natural disasters. God told his prophet Jeremiah

"'I will send war, hunger, and disease against them.'"

—Jeremiah 24:10 NCV

The drought and other disasters that ruined the Israelites' crops were sent for the purpose of bringing them to repentance—causing them to change their hearts and minds, and turning them back to God, as he told them through his prophet Amos:

"'I held back the rain from you three months before harvest time. . . . People weak from thirst went from town to town for water, but they could not get enough to drink. Still you did not come back to me,' says the LORD. 'I made your crops die from disease and mildew. When your gardens and your vineyards got larger, locusts ate your fig and olive trees. But still you did not come back to me,' says the LORD. 'I sent disasters against you, as I did to Egypt.'"

—Amos 4:7-10 NCV

The prophet Jeremiah elaborates on the sins of the people that prompted God to send disasters upon them:

"The land of Judah is full of people who are guilty of adultery. Because of this, the LORD cursed the land. It has become a very sad place, and the pastures have dried up. The people are evil and use their power in the wrong way. 'Both the prophets and the priests live as if there were no God. I have found them doing evil things even in my own Temple,' says the LORD. 'So they will be in danger. They will be forced into darkness where they will be defeated. I will bring disaster on them in the year I punish them,' says the LORD."

—Jeremiah 23:10-12 NCV

There is a popular notion today that it was only the God of the Old Testament who sent plagues and disasters, and that in the New Testament somehow a kind and gentle Jesus took the place of the mean Old Testament God. But that notion is popular only among people who don't actually read the New Testament. If they read it, they would realize that Jesus is just like his heavenly Father. Jesus said, "Whoever has seen me has seen the Father." (John 14:9 NCV) And Hebrews 1:3 says that Jesus is "the exact representation" of God the Father. (NIV)

When he healed a sick man who had been unable to walk, Jesus also told him to stop sinning, or something worse may happen to him:

"Later Jesus found him at the temple and said to him, 'See, you are well again. Stop sinning or something worse may happen to you.'"

—John 5:14 NIV

When the resurrected and risen Christ sent a message to the Christian church in the ancient city of Thyatira he gave them a stern warning of the punishment he would send on church members who behave immorally:

"I have this against you: You tolerate that woman Jezebel, who calls herself a prophetess. By her teaching she misleads my servants into sexual immorality and the eating of food sacrificed to idols. I have given her time to repent of her immorality, but she is unwilling. So I will cast her on a bed of suffering, and I will make those who commit adultery with her suffer intensely, unless they repent of her ways. I will strike her children dead. Then all the churches will know that I am he who searches hearts and minds, and I will repay each of you according to your deeds."

—Revelation 2:20-23 NIV

That was Jesus speaking—the same Jesus who taught love and forgiveness. The Apostle Paul spoke of "the kindness and sternness of God" (Romans 11:22 NIV)—kindness to those who accept the forgiveness of their sins and learn from God's mercy to leave sin behind and walk in God's ways, but sternness to those who disregard God's mercy and persist in wrongdoing.

So the revelation of God through Jesus Christ is consistent with the revelation of God in the Old Testament. He is a loving heavenly Father, but also an old-fashioned strict Father who corrects and disciplines people with the aim of bringing them to repentance. And he is a God who will ultimately punish with severity wrongdoers who reject his mercy.

The popular "Jesus" who loves and accepts everyone and everything, without a call to repentance, is not the real Jesus—the Jesus of the Bible. People who read the Bible from cover to cover find it to be consistent from cover to cover, because God does not change. In the book of Malachi, the last book of the Old Testament in most Bibles, God tells the prophet, "I am the LORD, and I do not change." (Malachi 3:6 NLT) And in the New Testament we are told, "Jesus Christ is the same yesterday and today and forever." (Hebrews 13:8 NIV)

Jesus warned that there would be natural disasters in the days leading up to his return in power:

". . . distress of nations in perplexity because of the roaring of the sea and the waves, people fainting with fear and with foreboding of what is coming on the world. . . . And then they will see the Son of Man coming in a cloud with power and great glory. Now when

these things begin to take place, straighten up and raise your heads, because your redemption is drawing near."

—Luke 21:25-28

When speaking of the days leading up to his second coming, Jesus also spoke of "famines and earthquakes in various places." (Matthew 24:7 NIV)

But, would these always be naturally occurring events, or would God actually send some of the disasters in the final days of this world?

The best answer is found in the New Testament's last book, the Apocalypse or Revelation. It speaks plainly of God sending plagues or disasters upon this rebellious world:

"There were seven angels bringing seven disasters. These are the last disasters, because after them, God's anger is finished."

—Revelation 15:1 NCV

These "last disasters" God would send through his angels would include "great heat" from the sun, which could be a reference to climate change and global warming:

"The fourth angel poured out his bowl on the sun, and he was given power to burn the people with fire. They were burned by the great heat, and they cursed the name of God, who had control over these disasters. But the people refused to change their hearts and lives and give glory to God."

—Revelation 16:8-9 NCV

The disasters during the end times would also affect sea life, reminiscent of recent reports of depleted fishing stocks and endangered species in the marine environment:

"A third of the sea turned into blood, a third of the living creatures in the sea died."

—Revelation 8:8-9 NIV

These end times disasters serve as warning signs, for the purpose of alerting people to the approaching end, and to call them to repent and return to God. But God knew ahead of time that many would refuse to listen:

"The other people who were not killed by these terrible disasters still did not change their hearts . . . and turn away from murder or evil magic, from their sexual sins or stealing."

—Revelation 9:20-21 NCV

So, if many people today who "believe in God" don't believe that God sends natural disasters, the reason may be that they don't believe in the God of the

Old and New Testaments, the God of the Bible—or that they are unfamiliar with what the Bible says about natural disasters in the final days of this world.

Anti-Semitism Foretold in Scripture

Hatred of the Jews is so common that a word has been coined to describe it. It is called "anti-Semitism"—a term recognized worldwide. But was hatred of the Jews actually foretold in the Bible?

Yes. According to the prophet Jeremiah, God said,

"'I will make them hated by all the kingdoms of the earth. People will curse them . . .'"

—Jeremiah 29:18 NCV

Is there any other nationality that has been the object of such hostility and disdain everywhere? The Irish have experienced poor treatment at the hands of the English, but the Irish are not looked down upon elsewhere. Koreans have been slighted in Japan, but don't face similar prejudice elsewhere. Blacks have been discriminated against in the American South, but are not universally scorned worldwide.

Yet the Jews have faced pogroms in Russia, expulsion from Spain, expulsion from ancient Rome, and expulsion from other nations. When the Apostle Paul was in Corinth, Greece, he met a Jewish Christian couple named Priscilla and Aquila, "who had recently come from Italy . . . because [Emperor] Claudius had ordered all Jews to leave Rome." (Acts 18:2 NIV) Between the years 1182 and 1394, various French kings expelled the Jews from their domains on multiple occasions. British King Edward I expelled all the Jews from England in the year 1290, and they were not officially readmitted until 1656. In 1492, the same year Christopher Columbus arrived at North America, the royal couple who commissioned his journey of exploration—Ferdinand and Isabella—expelled all the Jews from Spain. Dozens of other nations and jurisdictions have driven out their Jewish populations over the centuries.

The Jewish people have faced discrimination in America, persecution in Europe, as well as universal hostility worldwide.

Is that simply a coincidence? Or, is it a fulfillment of Bible prophecy?

As discussed elsewhere in this book, prophecies in both the Old Testament and the New Testament foretold that the Jewish people would be uprooted from their homeland and scattered worldwide:

"But it shall come about, if you do not obey the LORD your God . . . the LORD will scatter you among all peoples, from one end of the earth to the other end of the earth."

The Jews would be scattered worldwide according to the prophecies—only to be re-gathered to the land of Israel shortly before the end of the world. But what would happen to them in the meantime? The same prophecies also speak about the circumstances the Jews would face during the years of their dispersion among the nations.

Moses foretold that the rest of the people of the world would be hostile toward the Jews, making fun of them, ridiculing them and mocking them:

"You will become an object of horror, ridicule, and mockery among all the nations to which the LORD sends you."

—Deuteronomy 28:37 NLT

And the passage from Jeremiah partially quoted above explains that God told the prophet,

"'I will pursue them with the sword, famine and plague and will make them abhorrent to all the kingdoms of the earth and an object of cursing and horror, of scorn and reproach, among all the nations where I drive them.'"

—Jeremiah 29:18 NIV

Because their ancestors disregarded God and refused to obey him, the Jews faced a great Tribulation of hostility and persecution lasting many centuries.

Is there a lesson in this for the rest of us? The Apostle Paul wrote concerning "the severity of God" in punishing his Chosen People. (Romans 11:22 NIV) Scripture also foretells that he will soon redeem them and punish those who mistreated them, bringing judgment against the rest of mankind. Now is the time to repent.

The Holocaust Foretold in Scripture?

During the Second World War the Nazi government of Adolph Hitler carried out what it called "the Final Solution" for the Jewish problem, and what others have since called "the Holocaust." Over a period of three and a half years Hitler operated death camps that he set up for the specific purpose of exterminating the Jewish people. Six million Jews were killed.

The camp at Chelmno, Poland—the first concentration camp built exclusively to kill everyone sent there—was established in November, 1941, and mass murder began there on December 8, 1941. The last death camp, Mauthausen, was liberated three and a half years later in May, 1945. (Concentration camps set up to house Jews existed before this, but camps set up specifically to carry out genocide were operational for just three and a half years.)

Centuries earlier the prophet Daniel had foretold that an exceptionally cruel foreign ruler would hurt and kill the Jewish people over a period of three and a half years. Did the Bible foretell the Holocaust?

Daniel lived around twenty-five centuries ago, but he received a series of visions and messages from angels sent by God to tell him about what would happen to his people, the Jews, in the distant future:

"'Now I have come to explain to you what will happen to your people in the future, for the vision concerns a time yet to come.'"

—Daniel 10:14 NIV

He was told to

"'seal up the vision, for it concerns the distant future.'"

—Daniel 8:26 NIV

God's messengers told Daniel there would be "a time of distress such as has not happened from the beginning of nations until then" from which "your people . . . will be delivered." (Daniel 12:1 NIV)

"'When the end comes near for those kingdoms, a bold and cruel king who tells lies will come. This will happen when many people have turned against God. This king will be very powerful, but his power will not come from himself. He will cause terrible destruction and will be successful in everything he does. He will destroy powerful people and even God's holy people. This king

will succeed by using lies and force. He will think that he is very important. He will destroy many people without warning . . .'"

Does that description fit the Nazi regime of Adolph Hitler that blitzkrieged its way across Europe and attempted to exterminate the prophet Daniel's people?

In a related passage the angelic messenger God sent to Daniel told him,

"'This king will speak against the Most High God, and he will hurt and kill God's holy people. He will try to change times and laws that have already been set. The holy people that belong to God will be in that king's power for three and one-half years.'"

—Daniel 7:25 NCV

The angel also indicated that shortly after those three and a half years, the Jewish people would have their own nation restored—they would receive power to rule themselves again. The cruel ruler who was killing the Jews would be

"making war against God's holy people and was defeating them until God, who has been alive forever, came. He judged in favor of the holy people who belong to the Most High God; then the time came for them to receive the power to rule."

—Daniel 7:21-22 NCV

Daniel does not speak of them first as a "nation," but rather as a "people"— which would fit the circumstances of the Jews at the time of the Holocaust. In fact, it was shortly after the Holocaust that the nation of Israel was restored in 1948, and the holy people of the prophet Daniel were able to rule over the Promised Land for the first time in nearly two thousand years.

Was this what the prophet had been told would happen?

Demonic enemies of God tried to block their restoration to the Promised Land by annihilating the Jewish people. That attempt was implemented through what the Nazis called the "Final Solution" and what we today call the Holocaust. God, who sees the future, appears to have foretold this significant event though his inspired human prophets, and had those prophecies recorded in Scripture.

"Then another king will arise, more brutal than the other ten, and will destroy three of them. He will defy the Most High God, and wear down the saints [the Jews] with persecution, and try to change all laws, morals, and customs. God's people will be helpless in his hands for three and a half years."

—Daniel 7:24-25 LB

The Nazi "Third Reich" fits this description, and its extermination camps operated for three and a half years. Old Testament writers used the term "saints" (Hebrew *kodesh* = 'holy' or 'set apart') to refer to the Jews. At Mount Sinai, according to Moses, God gave his law to the "saints." (Deut. 33:2) King David called true-worshipping Jews of his day "the saints who are on the earth." (Ps. 16:2 NKJV)

In this case the prophet Daniel was given visions of "what will happen to your people in the days to come" (Dan. 10:14 *Jerusalem Bible*), including "a time of distress such as has not happened from the beginning of nations until then" from which "your people . . . will be delivered." (Dan 12:1 NIV) So, when Daniel used the term "saints," he had in mind God's 'holy people'—Daniel's own people, the Jews.

The New Testament book of Revelation seems to include a parallel of Daniel's Old Testament prophecy. Consider this possible interpretation [in brackets] of Revelation, chapter 12, which also speaks of three and a half years:

[1]**And there appeared a great wonder in heaven; a woman** [= Israel - Isa. 54:1,5,6; Jer. 3:14; 31:31,32] **clothed with the sun, and the moon under her feet, and upon her head a crown of twelve stars** [= the twelve tribes - Rev. 7:4-8]**:**

[2]**And she being with child cried, travailing in birth, and pained to be delivered.** [3] **And there appeared another wonder in heaven; and behold a great red dragon** [= Satan the devil - Rev. 12:9], **having seven heads and ten horns, and seven crowns upon his heads.** [4] **And his tail drew the third part of the stars of heaven, and did cast them to the earth: and the dragon stood before the woman which was ready to be delivered, for to devour her child as soon as it was born.**

[5] **And she brought forth a man child** [= Christ, the Messiah - Rom. 9:3-5], **who was to rule all nations with a rod of iron: and her child was caught up unto God, and to his throne.** [= After his death and resurrection, the Messiah ascended into heaven - Dan. 7:13]

[6] **And the woman fled into the wilderness** [= Israel was dispersed among all the nations, from one end of the earth to the other, including the Americas, land that was an unknown wilderness to Bible writers. - Deut. 28:64], **where she hath a place prepared of God, that they should feed her there a thousand two hundred and threescore days.** [To preserve Israel from complete annihilation during the Holocaust. 1260 days = 3 ½ years]

[7] **And there was war in heaven: Michael and his angels fought against the dragon; and the dragon fought and his angels,** [8] **And prevailed not; neither was their place found any more in heaven.** [9] **And the great dragon was cast out, that old serpent, called the**

Devil, and Satan, which deceiveth the whole world: he was cast out into the earth, and his angels were cast out with him. [Since this was invisible to human eyes, the timing would be uncertain, but apparently after Messiah's resurrection and before the Tribulation on Israel that began in 70 A.D.]

¹⁰ **And I heard a loud voice saying in heaven, Now is come salvation, and strength, and the kingdom of our God, and the power of his Christ: for the accuser of our brethren is cast down, which accused them before our God day and night. ¹¹ And they overcame him by the blood of the Lamb, and by the word of their testimony; and they loved not their lives unto the death. ¹² Therefore rejoice, ye heavens, and ye that dwell in them. Woe to the inhabiters of the earth and of the sea! for the devil is come down unto you, having great wrath, because he knoweth that he hath but a short time.**

¹³ **And when the dragon saw that he was cast unto the earth, he persecuted the woman** [= Israel] **which brought forth the man child.** [The dragon Satan had the Roman Empire subdue a Jewish rebellion, killing more than a million Jews, and scattering the rest throughout the Empire.]

⁴ **And to the woman were given two wings of a great eagle, that she might fly into the wilderness, into her place, where she is nourished for a time, and times, and half a time** [= 3 1/2 years], **from the face of the serpent.** [The scattering of the Jews served to preserve Israel from complete annihilation then and during the Tribulation's climax later in the 3 1/2 year Holocaust.]

⁵ **And the serpent cast out of his mouth water as a flood** [= the evil Nazi regime; compare Isa. 57:20] **after the woman, that he might cause her to be carried away of the flood. ¹⁶ And the earth helped the woman,** [Britain/America came to the rescue of the Jewish people] **and the earth opened her mouth, and swallowed up the flood** [= defeated the Nazi regime and stopped the Holocaust] **which the dragon cast out of his mouth.**

¹⁷ **And the dragon was wroth with the woman, and went to make war with the remnant of her seed, which keep the commandments of God, and have the testimony of Jesus Christ.** [= persecution of Christians that has intensified worldwide.]

—Revelation 12 KJV

Does the interpretation in the brackets above truly show a parallel between the Revelation and Daniel's prophecy? Readers must judge for themselves, until the day when God makes all these things clear to everyone.

During the 1800's and early 1900's advocates of "substitution theology" applied many of the prophecies about "Israel" to the Church instead of to the

Jews. So, when the Holocaust and the subsequent restoration of the state of Israel occurred, they missed any significance of these events as fulfillment of Bible prophecy.

But, if Daniel and the Revelation indeed foretold these events of recent history, then the remaining prophecies are well on track toward fulfillment—and all who are alive today do well to pay attention.

Jerusalem, Canaan, Sodom and Today's World

Are the events surrounding Jerusalem, Israel and the United Nations the only indications that the time is near for God's foretold intervention to bring an end to this world? Far from it! A close look at God's past interventions in human affairs sheds light on what is about to happen now. So, let's look at some of them:

Around 600 B.C., the ancient city of Jerusalem was destroyed.

Around 1400 B.C. the inhabitants of the land of Canaan were wiped out.

Around 1900 B.C. the cities of Sodom and Gomorrah were destroyed.

In each case, it was the God of the Bible who intervened and put a stop to the course that humans were taking. Different means were used each time. Jerusalem was destroyed by forces of the Babylonian empire. God used the armies of Israel to exterminate the Canaanites. Sodom and Gomorrah were annihilated by fire and sulfur raining down from the sky.

Why did God decree the destruction of Jerusalem, Sodom and Gomorrah, and the Canaanites? What did all those people do to provoke God's anger? Is today's world doing similar things that will provoke God's anger and bring about Divine intervention again, and this world's destruction?

JERUSALEM

Through the prophet Jeremiah, God listed his complaints against the people of Jerusalem and Judah.

They were worshiping false gods and practicing sexual immorality:

"The LORD said, 'Tell me why I should forgive you. Your children have left me and have made promises to idols that are not gods at all. I gave your children everything they needed, but they still were like an unfaithful wife to me. They spent much time in houses of prostitutes. They are like well-fed horses filled with sexual desire; each one wants another man's wife. Shouldn't I punish the people of Judah for doing these things?' says the LORD. 'Shouldn't I give a nation such as this the punishment it deserves?'"

—Jeremiah 5:7-9 NCV

They were committing adultery, misusing power, and acting as if God Almighty did not exist:

"The land of Judah is full of people who are guilty of adultery. . . The people are evil and use their power in the wrong way. 'Both the prophets and the priests live as if there were no God. I have found them doing evil things even in my own Temple,' says the LORD."

—Jeremiah 23:10-11 NCV

The people had strayed so far from God's law that there were even

"male prostitutes who were in the Temple of the LORD."

—2 Kings 23:7

They were exploiting the poor and proudly flaunting their sexuality:

"'Your houses are full of what you took from the poor. What gives you the right to crush my people and grind the faces of the poor into the dirt?' The LORD God All-Powerful says this. The LORD says, 'The women of Jerusalem are proud. They walk around with their heads held high, and they flirt with their eyes. They take quick, short steps, making noise with their ankle bracelets.'"

—Isaiah 3:14-16 NCV

For all of these reasons, God Almighty sent the armies of Babylon to destroy Jerusalem and send its people into captivity. Are the same sorts of things being done in our world today? Does God feel the same way about it? Won't he act in similar fashion to destroy this world that offends him?

SODOM AND GOMORRAH

Nearly four thousand years ago, many long centuries before Jerusalem was destroyed, there was another act of Divine intervention. At that time God rained down fire and sulfur from the sky to destroy the cities of Sodom and Gomorrah. His view of their inhabitants was expressed this way:

"Now the men of Sodom were wicked and were sinning greatly against the LORD." —Genesis 13:13 NIV

"Because the outcry against Sodom and Gomorrah is great, and because their sin is very grave," God considered destroying those cities. But first he sent two angels in the form of men to investigate, and he discussed the matter with Abraham. Abraham begged God not to "destroy the righteous with the wicked," and God agreed that he would spare the whole city of Sodom if he found ten good people there. (Gen. 18:17-32 NKJV)

Part of Abraham's concern must have been due to the fact that his nephew Lot was then living in Sodom. In fact, when the investigating angels arrived that evening, it was Lot who invited them to spend the night at his house. But the other inhabitants of the city soon expressed themselves:

"But before they lay down, the men of the city, the men of Sodom, surrounded the house, both young and old, all the people from every quarter. They called to Lot, and said to him, 'Where are the men who came in to you this night? Bring them out to us, that we may have sex with them.'" —Genesis 19:4-5

Instead of allowing this to happen, the angels blinded the rape mob, and in the morning they led Lot and his immediate family to safety outside the city limits, so that God could destroy the place.

"Then the LORD rained upon Sodom and upon Gomorrah brimstone and fire from the LORD out of heaven; And he overthrew those cities, and all the plain, and all the inhabitants of the cities, and that which grew upon the ground." —Genesis 19:24-25 KJV

Our modern English words 'sodomy' and 'sodomize' come from the name of that ancient city of Sodom that God destroyed as punishment for its inhabitants' sins.

CANAAN

Centuries after the destruction of Sodom, God led the people of Israel out of Egypt and into the Promised Land. But the Promised Land was not empty. It was the land of Canaan, populated by several national groups that were sentenced to annihilation because of their conduct that God condemned. The Israelites were commanded to kill the Canaanites, as God's executioners, and they were told, "you must not do as they do in the land of Canaan, where I am bringing you. Do not follow their customs." (Lev. 28:3 NCV) What customs? God told the Israelites,

"'You must never have sexual relations with your close relatives . . . You must not have sexual relations with your brother's wife . . . You must not have sexual relations with your neighbor's wife . . . You must not have sexual relations with a man as you would a woman. That is a hateful sin. You must not have sexual relations with an animal; it is not natural.'" —Leviticus 18:6, 16, 20, 22-23 NCV

God explained to the people of Israel,

"'The people who lived in the land before you did all these hateful things'"

—Leviticus 18:27 NCV

And that was why God was wiping them out and giving their land to the Jews.

But God has reformed since then, hasn't he? He wouldn't destroy people like that again, would he? The Christian New Testament warns us that God will again execute the same sort of punishment against those who persist in practicing sexual immorality—even referring back to God's destruction of Sodom and Gomorrah as an example. The Apostle Peter wrote that God

"condemned the cities of Sodom and Gomorrah by burning them to ashes, and made them an example of what is going to happen to the ungodly." —2 Peter 2:6 NIV

The Christian disciple Jude wrote similarly, pointing out clearly the sexual nature of the sins practiced by the inhabitants of those cities, and that they serve as a warning, an example of punishment to come:

"In a similar way, Sodom and Gomorrah and the surrounding towns gave themselves up to sexual immorality and perversion. They serve as an example of those who suffer the punishment of eternal fire." —Jude 7 NIV

Like the Old Testament, the Christian New Testament plainly spells out the specific types of sexual conduct that God condemns. The Apostle Paul wrote this to the Christian church in Rome:

"Therefore God also gave them up in the lusts of their hearts to uncleanness, that their bodies should be dishonored among themselves, who exchanged the truth of God for a lie, and worshiped and served the creature rather than the Creator, who is blessed forever. Amen.

"For this reason, God gave them up to vile passions. For their women changed the natural function into that which is against nature.

"Likewise also the men, leaving the natural function of the woman, burned in their lust toward one another, men doing what is inappropriate with men, and receiving in themselves the due penalty of their error.

"Even as they refused to have God in their knowledge, God gave them up to a reprobate mind, to do those things which are not fitting; being filled with all unrighteousness, sexual immorality, wickedness, covetousness . . . who, knowing the ordinance of God, that those who practice such things are worthy of death, not only do the same, but also approve of those who practice them."

—Romans 1:24-32

So, God's attitude toward this sort of behavior remained the same throughout the Old Testament and New Testament eras spanning thousands of years. What reason would there be to think that he may have changed his view now, simply because these forms of sexual conduct have become popular and accepted in today's world?

And what about our modern world's view of divorce—for any reason or no reason at all? The prophet Malachi expressed God's view when he wrote,

". . . the LORD sees how you treated the wife you married when you were young. You broke your promise to her, even though she was your partner and you had an agreement with her. God made husbands and wives to become one body and one spirit for his purpose—so they would have children who are true to God. So be careful, and do not break your promise to the wife you married when you were young. The LORD God of Israel says, 'I hate divorce. And I hate people who do cruel things as easily as they put on clothes,' says the LORD All-Powerful. So be careful. And do not break your trust."

—Malachi 2:14-16 NCV

And Jesus expressed the same view. He referred back to the first marriage in Genesis as the pattern God intended for mankind to follow:

"'Haven't you read that he who made them from the beginning made them male and female, and said, "For this cause a man shall leave his father and mother, and shall join to his wife; and the two shall become one flesh?" So that they are no more two, but one flesh. What therefore God has joined together, don't let man tear apart.'"

—Matthew 19:4-6

Jesus added,

"'Moses, because of the hardness of your hearts, allowed you to divorce your wives, but from the beginning it has not been so. I tell you that whoever divorces his wife, except for sexual immorality, and marries another, commits adultery; and he who marries her when she is divorced commits adultery.'"

—Matthew 19:8-9

Has God changed his mind about sexual conduct today? Did the 'sexual revolution' of the 1960's cause God to be more tolerant of sex outside of marriage, divorce without biblical grounds, and adultery? Has the 'gay pride' movement of recent decades caused God to change his mind about homosexual relations?

God does not change. He tells us,

"'I the LORD do not change.'"

—Malachi 3:6 NIV

"God is not a man, that he should lie, nor a son of man, that he should change his mind."

—Numbers 23:19 NIV

So, he must feel the same way about the same sorts of provocations that prompted him to act in the past. Looking at his past interventions should give us clues as to the timing of the coming apocalypse.

"Chosen People"—Chosen for What?

"Who are God's chosen people?" "The Jews." Ask almost anyone that question, and that is the answer you will receive. (However, many people will be quick to add their personal objection, qualifying statement, opinion or argument.) The expression "chosen people" is commonplace, part of everyone's vocabulary. And it is commonly known that the Bible applies this term to the Jews.

But what does it really mean?

First, it is important to understand what it definitely does NOT mean. It is clear from Scripture that their being the chosen people does not mean that God approves of everything they do or endorses the policies of their government. (See the chapter titled "Bible Prophecies Don't Endorse Israel's Behavior" earlier in this book.) In fact, the Jewish people come in for more criticism in the Bible than any other nationality. This criticism and condemnation spans much of Scripture, from the Old Testament's second book, Exodus, to the Gospels and letters in the New Testament.

According to Exodus they rebelled against God immediately after they had received the Ten Commandments, and so when Moses went up into Mt. Sinai to talk with God, God told Moses,

"'Go down, because your people, whom you brought up out of Egypt, have become corrupt. They have been quick to turn away from what I commanded them . . . I have seen these people . . . and they are a stiff-necked people. Now leave me alone so that my anger may burn against them and that I may destroy them.' . . . Then the LORD relented and did not bring on his people the disaster he had threatened."

—Exodus 32:7-14 NIV

Jesus spoke similarly when he mourned over the people of Jerusalem who had rejected the messages of the earlier prophets and who were about to reject him as the Messiah:

"'O Jerusalem, Jerusalem, you who kill the prophets and stone those sent to you, how often I have longed to gather your children together, as a hen gathers her chicks under her wings, but you were not willing.'"

—Matthew 23:37 NIV

Later the Apostle Paul, himself a Jew, faced violent opposition from his fellow Jews when trying to preach the Gospel message to non-Jews in the cities of Greece and Asia Minor, and so he referred to his own people as

"the Jews who killed the Lord Jesus and the prophets and also drove us out. They displease God and are hostile to everyone in their effort to keep us from speaking to the Gentiles so that they may be saved. In this way they always heap up their sins to the limit."

—1 Thessalonians 2:14-16 NIV

So, there is no basis for anyone to claim the Bible to be biased or slanted in favor of the Jews. Both the Old Testament and the New Testament feature more criticism of the Jews than of any other group of people.

So, in what way, then, are the Jews God's 'chosen people'?

The answer is found in the Bible, and, although the story begins thousands of years ago, it is essential to understanding what is happening today in the Middle East and its significance for the whole world.

When the first human pair, Adam and Eve, were expelled from the Garden of Eden, they went on to fulfill God's mandate to them to 'be fruitful and multiply and fill the earth.' (Genesis 1:28) Their offspring spread abroad and populated the planet, but, for the most part, they too followed the sinful course of their parents, and the earth was full of violence and immorality. The Creator returned to his creation to correct the mess they were making of the earth and to correct the course that these creatures endowed with free will had chosen for themselves. He announced that he would wipe the earth clean and start over again. He commissioned a righteous man named Noah to make this announcement and to provide the means for a new start for the world's repopulation via his offspring.

Noah spent perhaps a hundred and twenty years building, with the aid of his three sons, a floating box or ark that would preserve the lives of his family, his wife and sons and their wives. Then God sent the global deluge that wiped out the rest of mankind and cleansed the earth. After many months of floating over the flooded planet, Noah and his family finally disembarked when the flood waters had drained off the land. God caused geological processes to lower the ocean floors and raise the mountains and redistribute the water, and "the ark came to rest on the mountains of Ararat" in eastern Turkey. (Genesis 8:4 Jerusalem Bible)

As generations passed, the offspring of Noah increased in numbers and grew to a sizeable population. But, instead of spreading out to fill the earth as God intended, they remained concentrated in "the land of Shinar" not far from where the ark had settled after the flood. They set about building a city there. "Then they said, 'Come, let us build ourselves a city, and a tower with its top in the heavens, and let us make a name for ourselves, lest we be scattered abroad upon the face of the whole earth.'" (Genesis 11:2, 4 RSV)

They were able to do this, in part, because all mankind, descended from Noah and his sons, naturally spoke the same language. So, God intervened creatively by giving the people different languages, thus preventing them from continuing their cooperative venture, and forcing them to spread out and fill the earth.

As they moved apart and settled in widely scattered areas, the families of mankind all had opportunity to carry with them the knowledge passed on by their ancestors concerning God's dealings with mankind. But most of them chose not to preserve this knowledge. Instead, they began making up fables and even making up gods for themselves, and crafting idols to worship instead of worshiping the Creator. As the Apostle Paul explained it to Roman Christians thousands of years later:

"The wrath of God is being revealed from heaven against all the godlessness and wickedness of men who suppress the truth by their wickedness, since what may be known about God is plain to them, because God has made it plain to them. For since the creation of the world God's invisible qualities—his eternal power and divine nature—have been clearly seen, being understood from what has been made, so that men are without excuse. For although they knew God, they neither glorified him as God nor gave thanks to him, but their thinking became futile and their foolish hearts were darkened. Although they claimed to be wise, they became fools and exchanged the glory of the immortal God for images made to look like mortal man and birds and animals and reptiles."

—Romans 1:18-23 NIV

However, not everyone chose to forget about the true God, the Creator of heaven and earth. Some continued to worship the true God. In the line of descent from Noah's son Shem there was eventually born a man named Abram. God spoke to Abram, and he listened obediently, even though God's instructions were to leave his relatives behind and move his own household to a foreign land he had never seen before.

God told Abram,

"Neither shall thy name any more be called Abram, but thy name shall be Abraham; for a father of many nations have I made thee. And I will make thee exceeding fruitful, and I will make nations of thee, and kings shall come out of thee. And I will establish my covenant between me and thee and thy seed after thee in their

generations for an everlasting covenant, to be a God unto thee, and to thy seed after thee."

—Genesis 17:5-7 KJV)

Abraham was to be a father of "many nations," not just of the Jews. Through his wife Sarah, Abraham begat Isaac, the father of Jacob, whose name was later changed to Israel. But, through Sarah's Egyptian maid Hagar (a practice considered acceptable in that culture), Abraham fathered Ishmael, and Ishmael became the progenitor of many of the peoples inhabiting the Middle East:

"This is the account of Abraham's son Ishmael, whom Sarah's maidservant, Hagar the Egyptian, bore to Abraham. These are the names of the sons of Ishmael, listed in the order of their birth: Nebaioth the firstborn of Ishmael, Kedar, Adbeel, Mibsam, Mishma, Dumah, Massa, Hadad, Tema, Jetur, Naphish and Kedemah. These were the sons of Ishmael, and these are the names of the twelve tribal rulers according to their settlements and camps. Altogether, Ishmael lived a hundred and thirty-seven years. He breathed his last and died, and he was gathered to his people. His descendants settled in the area from Havilah to Shur, near the border of Egypt, as you go toward Asshur. And they lived in hostility toward all their brothers."

—Genesis 25:12-18 NIV

This "hostility" has continued into our day, in the form of Arab opposition to the Jews and the state of Israel.

Later in life, after the death of his wife Sarah, Abraham took another wife, who bore him additional sons, the progenitors of other Arab tribes:

"Abraham took another wife, whose name was Keturah. She bore him Zimran, Jokshan, Medan, Midian, Ishbak and Shuah. Jokshan was the father of Sheba and Dedan; the descendants of Dedan were the Asshurites, the Letushites and the Leummites. The sons of Midian were Ephah, Epher, Hanoch, Abida and Eldaah. All these were descendants of Keturah."

—Genesis 25:1-4 NIV

These, too, settled areas and towns of the Middle East that came to bear their names.

Abraham's son Isaac became father to twin sons: Jacob and Esau.

Esau's offspring composed several clans who came to be called Edomites and who inhabited land south of Judea and the Dead Sea:

"These were the chiefs descended from Esau, by name, according to their clans and regions: Timna, Alvah, Jetheth, Oholibamah, Elah, Pinon, Kenaz, Teman, Mibzar, Magdiel and Iram. These were the chiefs of Edom, according to their settlements in the land they occupied. This was Esau the father of the Edomites."

—Genesis 36:40-43 NIV

Meanwhile, "Jacob lived in the land where his father had stayed, the land of Canaan." (Genesis 37:1 NIV) He fathered twelve sons by his two wives and two concubines. These sons, in turn, became the progenitors of the twelve tribes of Israel. But, first, due to a famine in the land of Canaan the whole family went to live in Egypt, where vast amounts of food had been put into storage ahead of time by Jacob's son Joseph who had been appointed prime minister of Egypt. (The whole story is fascinating and is found in the Bible book of Genesis.)

While living in Egypt for hundreds of years, Jacob's descendents grew into twelve populous tribes, so populous that the king of Egypt began to fear them and put them into slavery to keep them under control. (Exodus 1:9-11) God spoke to an Israelite named Moses and gave him the assignment of leading the people of Israel up out of Egypt. He also told Moses to tell them that they were his chosen people:

"For you are a people holy to the LORD your God. The LORD your God has chosen you out of all the peoples on the face of the earth to be his people, his treasured possession. The LORD did not set his affection on you and choose you because you were more numerous than other peoples, for you were the fewest of all peoples. But it was because the LORD loved you and kept the oath he swore to your forefathers that he brought you out with a mighty hand and redeemed you from the land of slavery, from the power of Pharaoh king of Egypt."

—Deuteronomy 7:6-8 NIV

From that point on, there has been jealousy and rivalry and war among these close relatives, the Arabs and the Israelites. It is a jealousy that goes beyond normal sibling rivalry. It revolves around choices God made and the promises he made to Israel as his chosen people.

Psychologists have written books about 'irregular people' and 'toxic parents' who favor one child over another unreasonably. Is that the sort of parent God was in choosing Jacob's offspring rather than Esau's?

No, God had sound reasons for his special dealings with the nation of Israel. And he engineered things so that the Jews did not, ultimately, have an unfair advantage over the rest of mankind. Their being 'chosen' resulted in many blessings, but also in many tribulations. What other nationality has been persecuted from one country to another, culminating in a holocaust in which six million were killed? When faced with such persecution, the lead character in the play Fiddler on the Roof finds it so painful that he asks God to 'choose someone else next time.'

But why did God 'choose' one people out of all mankind? Primarily, because the Messiah would need to be born in a community that would be able to receive him appropriately. By the time the Christ child was scheduled to be born, the rest of mankind had forgotten about the Creator and his promised "seed." (More will be said about the Promised Seed in the next chapter of this book.) The Jews would have forgotten, too, and would have been worshiping idols with the rest of the human race, if God had not intervened and made them his Chosen People.

When Moses was still on the mountain receiving the Ten Commandments from God, the people of Israel had his brother Aaron make them a golden calf and they bowed down and worshiped it. They turned to idolatry just as quickly as all the other nations. But God intervened and forced them to destroy that idol. The history of Israel shows that he intervened many, many times in the same way, because the people of Israel had the same sinful tendencies as the other nations to abandon true worship and to fall into idolatry.

The Chosen People were given the Ten Commandments, as well as more than six hundred laws of God, to force them to preserve true worship of the one living and true God, and to preserve some semblance of moral and ethical purity. God could have chosen any nationality to provide this appropriate framework to receive the Messiah. But, he had to choose somebody. So, why not the Jews?

Besides providing a society practicing true worship, in which the Messiah could make an appearance, God also needed a Chosen People to preserve the sacred Scriptures. A pagan society would not have valued the holy writings, and they would have been lost. So, one nation on the earth had to be kept somewhat on the straight and narrow, to act as custodians of the Bible.

"The Jews were entrusted with the whole revelation of God," according to the Apostle Paul. (Romans 3:2 New Living Translation) "The Jews are the people to whom God's message was entrusted." (Romans 3:2 Jerusalem Bible) Even the Islamic holy book the Koran says that the Jews "were required to preserve the Book of ALLAH" and that "they were guardians over it." (5:45)

So, the Jews were 'chosen' to do a job that needed to be done. Any nation could have been chosen, and if another nation had been instead of the Jews— say, the Irish, for example—then people would have asked, "Why the Irish?" in the same way that they now ask, "Why the Jews?"

Ultimately, though, the Jews were not given a permanent advantage over other nations, because God is not the sort of parent who plays favorites:

"There will be trouble and distress for every human being who does evil: first for the Jew, then for the Gentile; but glory, honor and peace for everyone who does good: first for the Jew, then for the Gentile. For God does not show favoritism."

—Romans 2:9-11 NIV

The Jews were the people 'chosen' to preserve true worship until the arrival of the Messiah, and the people 'chosen' to preserve the Sacred Scriptures with their inspired history and prophecy. But, God did this with the aim of saving other people who would later be 'chosen' from all nations. Because of the things that God accomplished in this way, personal salvation is now available to both Jews and non-Jews on the same basis:

"Is God the God of Jews only? Is he not the God of Gentiles too? Yes, of Gentiles too, since there is only one God, who will justify the circumcised by faith and the uncircumcised through that same faith."

—Romans 3:29-30 NIV

In fact, to avoid giving the Jews an unfair advantage over other nationalities, when it came to receiving blessings through the Messiah, God placed an obstacle in their path: "Blindness in part is happened to Israel, until the fulness of the Gentiles be come in," or "One section of Israel has become blind, but this will last only until the whole pagan world has entered." (Romans 11:25 KJV and Jerusalem Bible)

The Jews, too, would end up being blessed. But, in the meantime, they would have to suffer more than many other peoples. For example, they would undergo centuries of slavery: "And he said unto Abram, Know of a surety that thy seed shall be a stranger in a land [that is] not theirs, and shall serve them; and they shall afflict them four hundred years." (Gen 15:13 KJV) And, if they failed in their responsibilities to keep the strict laws God gave them, "the LORD will scatter you among all peoples, from one end of the earth to the other end of the earth." (Deut. 28:15, 64 NASB)

The Jews were 'chosen' to do a job that needed to be done, but it was a servant's job, because its aim was to bless the rest of mankind. The end result would be, as God told Abraham, "And in thy seed shall all the nations of the earth be blessed." (Gen 22:18 KJV)

Promised Seed

"And in thy seed shall all the nations of the earth be blessed," God told Abraham. (Gen 22:18 KJV) Who would that promised seed prove to be? The answer is not immediately obvious, because God used the term "seed" differently at different times. First, he used the term very broadly to refer to the vast numbers of people who would be descended from Abraham, but later God revealed that the blessings would come to "all the nations" from a single individual at the end of a long line of descent.

The Apostle Paul explained, "Now to Abraham and his seed were the promises made. He saith not, And to seeds, as of many; but as of one, And to thy seed, which is Christ." (Gal 3:16 KJV) Besides calling him the seed of Abraham, Paul also referred to Jesus as King David's seed: "Christ our Lord, which was made of the seed of David according to the flesh." (Romans 1:3 KJV)

What is the connection between Abraham and Christ? And between David and Christ? The Bible records these connections in the long chain of genealogies and histories found in the Old Testament. But the Gospel writer Matthew sums it up for us this way:

"A record of the genealogy of Jesus Christ the son of David, the son of Abraham:

Abraham was the father of Isaac,

Isaac the father of Jacob,

Jacob the father of Judah and his brothers,

Judah the father of Perez and Zerah, whose mother was Tamar,

Perez the father of Hezron,

Hezron the father of Ram,

Ram the father of Amminadab,

Amminadab the father of Nahshon,

Nahshon the father of Salmon,

Salmon the father of Boaz, whose mother was Rahab,

Boaz the father of Obed, whose mother was Ruth,

Obed the father of Jesse,

and Jesse the father of King David.

David was the father of Solomon, whose mother had been Uriah's wife,

Solomon the father of Rehoboam,

Rehoboam the father of Abijah,

Abijah the father of Asa,

Asa the father of Jehoshaphat,

Jehoshaphat the father of Jehoram,

Jehoram the father of Uzziah,

Uzziah the father of Jotham,

Jotham the father of Ahaz,

Ahaz the father of Hezekiah,

Hezekiah the father of Manasseh,

Manasseh the father of Amon,

Amon the father of Josiah,

and Josiah the father of Jeconiah and his brothers at the time of the exile to Babylon.

After the exile to Babylon:

Jeconiah was the father of Shealtiel,

Shealtiel the father of Zerubbabel,

Zerubbabel the father of Abiud,

Abiud the father of Eliakim,

Eliakim the father of Azor,

Azor the father of Zadok,

Zadok the father of Akim,

Akim the father of Eliud,

Eliud the father of Eleazar,

Eleazar the father of Matthan,

Matthan the father of Jacob,

and Jacob the father of Joseph, the husband of Mary, of whom was born Jesus, who is called Christ.

Thus there were fourteen generations in all from Abraham to David, fourteen from David to the exile to Babylon, and fourteen from the exile to the Christ."

—Matthew 1:1-17 NIV

On several occasions God indicated that Abraham's seed or offspring would grow to include vast numbers of people. "And I will make thy seed as the dust of the earth: so that if a man can number the dust of the earth, then shall thy seed also be numbered." (Gen 13:16 KJV) "And he brought him forth abroad, and said, Look now toward heaven, and tell the stars, if thou be able to number them: and he said unto him, So shall thy seed be." (Gen 15:5 KJV) The number would be literally astronomical, as the latter verse indicates.

In a general sense Abraham's seed would include all of his offspring, of course. But God made a distinction and indicated that the promises he gave to Abraham would apply to a certain line of descent. When a conflict developed between Abraham's young son Isaac, whom his wife Sarah had borne, and his older son Ishmael, his child through Sarah's servant Hagar, God instructed him to send Hagar and Ishmael away, as Sarah had requested:

"And God said unto Abraham, Let it not be grievous in thy sight because of the lad, and because of thy bondwoman; in all that Sarah hath said unto thee, hearken unto her voice; for in Isaac shall thy seed be called. And also of the son of the bondwoman will I make a nation, because he is thy seed."

—Genesis 21:12-13 KJV

God would cause a nation of people to descend from Ishmael, "because he is thy seed," but the promised blessings would come through Isaac, "for in Isaac shall thy seed be called." Or, as the New Living Translation puts it, "for Isaac is the son through whom your descendants will be counted." (Gen. 21:13) Or, "it is through Isaac that your offspring will be reckoned." (NIV) The promises of blessing were part of a covenant or formal agreement that God entered into with Abraham, and he indicated that he would continue his covenant with Isaac:

"And God said, Sarah thy wife shall bear thee a son indeed; and thou shalt call his name Isaac: and I will establish my covenant with him for an everlasting covenant, and with his seed after him."

—Genesis 17:19 KJV

There is no biblical record of God making a personal covenant with Ishmael, but the Almighty spoke to Isaac very much in the same way that he had spoken to Abraham: "And the LORD appeared unto him the same night, and said, I am the God of Abraham thy father: fear not, for I am with thee, and will bless thee, and multiply thy seed for my servant Abraham's sake." (Gen 26:24 KJV)

Likewise, when it came to Isaac's twin sons Jacob and Esau, the heavenly Father of all mankind chose one of them in connection with the promised seed. It was to Jacob that he said,

"And thy seed shall be as the dust of the earth, and thou shalt spread abroad to the west, and to the east, and to the north, and to the south: and in thee and in thy seed shall all the families of the earth be blessed."

—Genesis 28:14 KJV

These were not choices made on the spur of the moment, after Isaac was born and then, again, after Jacob was born. No, the One who sees the future and who knows the end from the beginning, knew ahead of time the line of descent that would produce the promised seed. He knew the destiny of the Israelites way back when he made his first promises to Abraham: "And he said unto Abram, Know of a surety that thy seed shall be a stranger in a land that is not theirs, and shall serve them; and they shall afflict them four hundred years." (Gen 15:13 KJV) God knew the future, not just of the nation of Israel, but also of the specific line of descent that would lead to the Messiah or Christ ("Anointed One" in Hebrew and Greek, respectively).

As can be seen in Matthew's genealogy, above, God selected a line of descent though King David. (Read the fascinating story of David in the Bible books of First and Second Samuel.) "I have made a covenant with my chosen, I have sworn unto David my servant, Thy seed will I establish for ever, and build up thy throne to all generations." (Psalm 89:3-4 KJV)

"Now then, tell my servant David, 'This is what the LORD Almighty says: I took you from the pasture and from following the flock to be ruler over my people Israel. . . . When your days are over and you rest with your fathers, I will raise up your offspring to succeed you, who will come from your own body, and I will establish his kingdom. He is the one who will build a house for my Name, and I will establish the throne of his kingdom forever. I will be his father, and he will be my son. ... Your house and your kingdom will endure forever before me; your throne will be established forever.'"

—2 Samuel 7:8-16 NIV

David's son Solomon succeeded him as king of Israel, and Solomon built the 'house' or temple of God in Jerusalem, as promised. And a long succession of kings in David's line ruled for hundreds of years. But God's promise to David hinted at more than that; it hinted at a descendent who would be called God's Son and who would rule as king forever.

After being given a vision outlining a succession of world powers that would encroach on the territory of Israel over a period of hundreds of years, the prophet Daniel was given another vision depicting this promised immortal ruler, the promised seed who would be born "like a son of man," yet who would have access to heaven and to the presence of God the Father:

"In my vision at night I looked, and there before me was one like a son of man, coming with the clouds of heaven. He approached the Ancient of Days and was led into his presence. He was given authority, glory and sovereign power; all peoples, nations and men of every language worshiped him. His dominion is an everlasting dominion that will not pass away, and his kingdom is one that will never be destroyed."

—Daniel 7:13-14 NIV

The prophet Isaiah provided additional details about the promised seed who would be born of a virgin and who would preach in Galilee: "Galilee" would "see a great Light" because "a virgin shall conceive, and bear a son." "For unto us a child is born, unto us a son is given: and the government shall be upon his shoulder: and his name shall be called Wonderful, Counsellor, The mighty God, The everlasting Father, The Prince of Peace." (Isaiah 7:14; 9:1-6 KJV)

The Messiah's birth would begin an era when many non-Jewish people of all the nations would turn for hope to "the root of Jesse, that standeth for an ensign for the peoples. Unto him shall the nations seek." (Isaiah 11:10 Jewish Publication Society of America) Isaiah was referring here to Jesus' descent from David, son of Jesse. The Apostle Paul made clear that Isaiah was prophesying about Christ, when Paul quoted him: "And again, Isaiah says, 'The Root of Jesse will spring up, one who will arise to rule over the nations; the Gentiles will hope in him.'" (Romans 15:12 NIV)

For more about prophecies identifying the Messiah and prophecies he has fulfilled, see the chapter of this book titled "Promised Messiah."

With millions of people of all nationalities putting faith in the Jewish Messiah and returning to the one living and true God, it is already true that, as God promised Abraham, "And in thy seed shall all the nations of the earth be blessed." (Gen 22:18 KJV) Even greater blessings for all mankind lie ahead when, as promised elsewhere in the Bible, Christ returns to rule the world from Jerusalem, the Holy City.

"Promised Land"—Promised to Whom?

Even in the vocabulary of unchurched people the expression "Promised Land" is synonymous with the land of Israel. Where did this expression come from?

Before God confused the languages and scattered the people at the tower of Babel, the world's human population was concentrated in the plain of Shinar near the Tigris and Euphrates rivers. After that, when the nations were scattered about to the four corners of the globe, those who spoke Hebrew still resided close to Shinar. But a small family group began to migrate southward.

"Terah took his son Abram, his grandson Lot son of Haran, and his daughter-in-law Sarai, the wife of his son Abram, and together they set out from Ur of the Chaldeans to go to Canaan. But when they came to Haran, they settled there."

—Genesis 11:31 NIV

Ur is the same town in modern Iraq where, on April 15, 2003, representatives of various Iraqi exile groups met under the auspices of the victorious United States military to begin talks aimed at forming a new government for Iraq. The ruins of Haran (also spelled Harran) are located in modern-day Turkey.

Abram, whom God renamed Abraham, was in his seventies and still living in Haran when God spoke to him and told him to leave the land of his relatives and to go to a new land that he would give him:

"Now the LORD had said unto Abram, Get thee out of thy country, and from thy kindred, and from thy father's house, unto a land that I will shew thee."

—Genesis 12:1 KJV

So, together with his wife Sarai and his nephew Lot and several dozen servants, Abram set out toward the eastern shore of the Mediterranean Sea.

God led Abraham to the land of Canaan, land that today is covered by the nations of Israel and Jordan. (Canaan was named after the forefather of its inhabitants, a grandson of Noah. "And the sons of Noah, that went forth of the ark, were Shem, and Ham, and Japheth. . . . And the sons of Ham; Cush, and Mizraim, and Phut, and Canaan." (Gen 9:18; 10:6 KJV)

The land was sparsely populated, so even the Canaanites felt that there was plenty of room for nomadic Abram and his nephew Lot. They had no way of knowing that God planned to transfer ownership of the land eventually to Abram's offspring.

"And Abram passed through the land unto the place of Sichem, unto the plain of Moreh. And the Canaanite was then in the land. And the LORD appeared unto Abram, and said, Unto thy seed will I give this land: and there builded he an altar unto the LORD, who appeared unto him."

—Genesis 12:6-7 KJV

After a while, the two patriarchs Abraham and Lot found it difficult to share pasture land, because their shepherds kept getting into arguments with each other. Abram and Lot discussed the situation and decided to separate. Abram told Lot to choose which pastures he wanted: the land to the north or the land to the south. Lot chose the land of 'the District,' the area around Sodom and Gomorrah. So, Abram headed in the opposite direction.

God appeared to Abram again and repeated the promise:

"And the LORD said unto Abram, after that Lot was separated from him, Lift up now thine eyes, and look from the place where thou art northward, and southward, and eastward, and westward: For all the land which thou seest, to thee will I give it, and to thy seed for ever."

—Genesis 13:14-15 KJV

Abraham's son Isaac and his grandson Jacob were born there, and God later appeared to Isaac and to Jacob and repeated to them the same promise regarding the land:

"God said to him, 'Your name is Jacob, but you will no longer be called Jacob; your name will be Israel.' So he named him Israel. And God said to him, 'I am God Almighty; be fruitful and increase in number. A nation and a community of nations will come from you, and kings will come from your body. The land I gave to Abraham and Isaac I also give to you, and I will give this land to your descendants after you.'"

—Genesis 35:10-12 NIV

Jacob raised twelve sons there but did not own the land. He merely dwelt in it as a visitor, an alien. When his older sons became jealous of the second-youngest son Joseph, they sold him into slavery to a caravan of travelers who, in turn, took him to Egypt and sold him there. In Egypt Joseph ended up in prison, but, through God's miraculous intervention, he came to be a servant of Pharaoh, the king of Egypt. It's a long story (worth reading in the Bible), but Pharaoh eventually put Joseph in charge of all his possessions so that Joseph was, in effect, the prime minister of Egypt.

Several years later there was a food shortage in the land where Jacob dwelt with his remaining sons, so he sent them to Egypt looking for food, and there they became re-united with Joseph. Joseph invited his father Jacob and his brothers to move to Egypt to live so that they would have food during the famine.

The offspring of Jacob, now named Israel, grew in great numbers in Egypt. They were so fertile and multiplied so fast that the Egyptians became afraid of their numbers and enslaved them to keep them under control. Finally God sent Moses to lead the Israelites up out of Egypt.

After sending in a dozen spies to report on what they found in the promised land of Canaan, most of the people lacked faith that God would give them victory over the Canaanites. They did not want to proceed. So, God had Moses lead them on a long, circuitous route through the wilderness for forty years, until that unfaithful generation had died off.

At the end of the forty years Moses was a hundred and twenty years old. God had him lead the Jews to the edge of the promised land, and then took him up to the top of a high mountain and showed him the land. "Then the LORD said to him, 'This is the land I promised on oath to Abraham, Isaac and Jacob when I said, "I will give it to your descendants." I have let you see it with your eyes, but you will not cross over into it.'" (Gen. 34:4 NIV) Moses died there, but only after appointing his deputy Joshua to lead the people in the conquest of Canaan.

"After the death of Moses the servant of the LORD, the LORD said to Joshua son of Nun, Moses' aide: 'Moses my servant is dead. Now then, you and all these people, get ready to cross the Jordan River into the land I am about to give to them—to the Israelites. I will give you every place where you set your foot, as I promised Moses. Your territory will extend from the desert to Lebanon, and from the great river, the Euphrates—all the Hittite country—to the Great Sea on the west. No one will be able to stand up against you all the days of your life. As I was with Moses, so I will be with you; I will never leave you nor forsake you. Be strong and courageous, because you will lead these people to inherit the land I swore to their forefathers to give them.'"

—Joshua 1:1-6 NIV

The land they were to conquer was a fruitful and productive land, but it was filled with inhabitants. The Canaanites were numerous and powerful. But they were a corrupt people who practiced child sacrifice and gross sexual immorality. God had passed judgment on them and had decided to execute them. And he appointed the people of Israel as his executioners.

Through Moses, God had told the Jews, "you must not do as they do in the land of Canaan, where I am bringing you. Do not follow their practices." Then he described those Canaanite practices as including "sexual relations with your mother . . . sexual relations with your sister," and even "sexual relations with an animal." He warned them against child sacrifice and the practice of homosexuality: "Do not give any of your children to be sacrificed. . . . Do not lie with a man as one lies with a woman; that is detestable." And then God explained that this was the way the people of Canaan had been living: "Do not defile yourselves in any of these ways, because this is how the nations that I am going to drive out before you became defiled. Even the land was defiled; so I punished it for its sin, and the land vomited out its inhabitants." God would apply the same standard to the Jews; if they took up living like the Canaanites, they would meet the Canaanites' fate: "And if you defile the land, it will vomit you out as it vomited out the nations that were before you." (Lev. 18:3-28 NIV)

So he instructed Joshua to enter the land of Canaan and lay siege to its cities, and to completely exterminate the people of the land. He was not to leave anyone alive. All were to be killed: men, women and children.

If a leader today were to conceive such a plan, it would be called genocide. But, as the Creator of mankind, God is the rightful judge. As the giver of life, he has the divine prerogative to set the limits of life and death, both for individuals and for whole nations. He is both just and justified in such actions. So, when the armies of Israel marched into land of Canaan and laid waste to its cities, this was not genocide. It was a judgment from God.

Besides exterminating the people, they were also to wipe out the artifacts of Canaanite worship, because it was a perverted form of false religion glorifying sexuality and perversion. Sacred poles were huge phallic symbols. Idols displayed grossly enlarged sex organs. "'Do not bow down before their gods or worship them or follow their practices. You must demolish them and break their sacred stones to pieces,'" God commanded. (Deut. 23:24 NIV)

Thus, God gave Israel the promised land, but keeping it was conditional on their obedience.

How did they fare? Biblical history reveals that Israel failed to carry out God's instructions. They compromised and allowed some of the Canaanites to remain alive, and they failed to exterminate their perverted religion. This failure to follow divine instructions completely would come back to haunt future generations. Men and women of Israel would be led astray to worship the Canaanite gods. Idolatry would keep rearing its head among the Israelites.

Israel too would lose the promised land for failure to keep God's covenant. He had told them through Moses that this is what would happen if they failed to keep their agreement with him. They would be removed from the land and be scattered throughout the earth. "But it shall come about, if you do not obey the LORD your God . . . the LORD will scatter you among all peoples, from one end of the earth to the other end of the earth." (Deut. 28:15, 64 NASB) And this is what eventually happened.

But, that did not mean they would lose the land permanently. God promised them that he would much later return them to the promised land: ". . . then the LORD thy God will turn thy captivity, and have compassion upon thee, and will return and gather thee from all the nations, whither the LORD thy God hath scattered thee . . . from thence will he fetch thee: And the LORD thy God will bring thee into the land which thy fathers possessed, and thou shalt possess it." (Deut. 30:3-5 KJV) ". . . the LORD will . . . assemble the dispersed of Israel, and gather together the scattered of Judah from the four corners of the earth." (Isaiah 11:11-12 The Holy Scriptures, Jewish Publication Society of America)

So the land of Israel was promised to the offspring of Jacob not just once, but also it was promised that the land would return to their possession at the time of the end. And this is the promise that began to be fulfilled when the state of Israel was re-established in 1948. But this was only the beginning of prophetic fulfillment regarding the promised land, because God promised that this land would belong to those people and their descendants forever under the rule of his Messiah, Jesus Christ.

Besides being a people assigned to preserve a written record of human history going back to the creation, and besides being a people kept separate to preserve the true worship of the true God, the Jews were also chosen to preserve the line of descent leading to the Messiah, Jesus Christ.

And their presence as a functioning Jewish state in the Promised Land at 'the time of the end' is essential for the fulfillment of the remaining prophecies concerning Christ's return. This is no coincidence. Rather, the God who predicted these events has the power to make sure that they will be fulfilled exactly as he said they would be.

"Holy City"

Unlike the expressions "chosen people" and "promised land," the term "holy city" does not find a universally accepted definition. Some people may apply the term to the Vatican or Rome, while others might apply it to Mecca, and still others may apply it to Abydos in Egypt, Nippur in Iraq, Lhasa in Tibet, Ujjain in India, or a host of other cities 'holy' to one sect or another.

Nevertheless, the most wide-spread use of the expression "holy city" has application to Jerusalem. Jerusalem is a holy city to three of the world's major religions: Judaism, Islam and Christianity. Its religious importance to so many of the people of the world has been cited in efforts to make it an international city under United Nations control. "The City of Jerusalem . . . shall be administered by the United Nations," according to U.N. General Assembly Resolution 181, enacted in 1947.

In biblical terms, Jerusalem is the only "holy city." It is referred to as such throughout both Old and New Testaments. "And the rulers of the people dwelt at Jerusalem: the rest of the people also cast lots, to bring one of ten to dwell in Jerusalem the holy city, and nine parts [to dwell] in [other] cities. . . . All the Levites in the holy city were two hundred fourscore and four." (Neh. 11:1, 18 KJV) "Awake, awake; put on thy strength, O Zion; put on thy beautiful garments, O Jerusalem, the holy city: for henceforth there shall no more come into thee the uncircumcised and the unclean." (Isa 52:1 KJV) "Then the devil taketh him up into the holy city, and setteth him on a pinnacle of the temple." (Matthew 4:5 KJV) ". . . and came out of the graves after his resurrection, and went into the holy city, and appeared unto many." (Matthew 27:53 KJV) See also Isaiah 48:2; Daniel 9:24; Mark 4:5; and Rev 11:2, 22:19.

This usage of the term is not simply due to familiarity with the location on the part of Bible writers, all of whom were Hebrews who spent most of their lives in the Middle East. It is due to a choice on God's part. The Creator's choice of this particular city was announced at the time of King David, who took the city out of the hands of its long-time inhabitants, the pagan Jebusites. The Almighty referred to it as, "Jerusalem, the city which I have chosen me to put my name there." (1Ki. 11:36 KJV) God specified, "I have chosen Jerusalem, that my name might be there; and have chosen David to be over my people Israel." (2 Chron. 6:6 KJV) It was there that God had King David place the holy tabernacle with its Ark of the Covenant. And there is where God told David he would have his temple built.

But that was not the beginning of Jerusalem as a center of true worship. The city's name means "foundation of peace" or "possession of peace," with the second part of the name—"salem"—derived from the same source as the Hebrew "shalom" and the Arabic "salam" or "salaam," both meaning "peace." The first mention of Jerusalem's existence is found in the book of Genesis, where it is referred to as "Salem." Abraham was living as an alien in the land God promised to him, when a marauding band led by the kings of several Canaanite cities swept down and took captive Abraham's nephew Lot. Abraham allied himself with the kings of some other nearby cities and, with a small military force, he defeated the hostile kings and rescued his nephew. At this point there appeared on the scene a man named Melchizedek who is identified as "king of Salem." He was also called "priest of the most high God," and he apparently led Abraham in a celebratory worship service, at the end of which Abraham tithed a tenth of the spoils of war to this priest. "And Melchizedek king of Salem brought forth bread and wine: and he was the priest of the most high God." (Gen 14:18 KJV)

Besides the account in Genesis, the writer of the letter to the Hebrews in the New Testament tells the same story: "For this Melchisedec, king of Salem, priest of the most high God, who met Abraham returning from the slaughter of the kings, and blessed him; To whom also Abraham gave a tenth part of all; first being by interpretation King of righteousness, and after that also King of Salem, which is, King of peace." (Hebrews 7:1-2 KJV)

There is no doubt that Salem and Jerusalem are one and the same, because the Psalmist refers to the holy city by its ancient name: "In Salem also is his tabernacle, and his dwelling place in Zion." (Psalm 76:2 KJV) So, under the priesthood of Melchizedek, Jerusalem was already a holy city and a center of true worship—at least as far back as the time of Abraham.

The next time we read about the city, it was inhabited by the Canaanite people called Jebusites. This was at the time of the Israeli invasion of the Promised Land under the leadership of Moses' successor Joshua. He had instructions from God to wipe out the corrupt inhabitants of the land and to empty their cities for settlement by the Jews, recently freed from Egyptian slavery. However, Joshua and his successors failed to carry out these instructions completely, and one of the cities they left inhabited by its pagan Canaanite population was the city of Jerusalem.

"As for the Jebusites the inhabitants of Jerusalem, the children of Judah could not drive them out: but the Jebusites dwell with the children of Judah at Jerusalem unto this day." (Joshua 15:63 KJV) "Now the children of Judah had fought against Jerusalem, and had taken it, and smitten it with the edge of the sword, and set the city on fire. . . . And the children of Benjamin did not drive out the Jebusites that inhabited Jerusalem; but the Jebusites dwell with the children of Benjamin in Jerusalem unto this day." (Judges 1:8, 21 KJV) The Jebusites continued to live there alongside the Israelites throughout the centuries of the Judges until the time of King David.

Through his prophet, God told David that he wanted his temple, which was then merely a portable tent or tabernacle, to reside in Jerusalem. The chief obstacle was the Jebusite fortress on a hill named Zion in the midst of the city. David defeated the Jebusites, and captured their "stronghold of Zion," which came to be known from then on as "the city of David." (2 Samuel 5:7 Jewish Publication Society) He had been ruling Israel from the town of Hebron, but now he moved into the city and made it his capital. "In Hebron he reigned over Judah seven years and six months: and in Jerusalem he reigned thirty and three years over all Israel and Judah." (2 Samuel 5:5 KJV) Some time later he also brought the Ark of the Covenant into the city, so that the tabernacle of worship resided in Jerusalem as well.

Later, David gave to his son Solomon the architectural plans for a more permanent temple of God to be built there in Jerusalem: "Then David gave his son Solomon the plans for the portico of the temple, its buildings, its storerooms, its upper parts, its inner rooms and the place of atonement. He gave him the plans of all that the Spirit had put in his mind for the courts of the temple of the LORD and all the surrounding rooms, for the treasuries of the temple of God and for the treasuries for the dedicated things." (1 Chron. 28:11-12 NIV) Some time after David's death, Solomon built that temple.

So, Jerusalem became the permanent center for Jewish worship of the one true God.

The Temple Mount was a separate hill, close by Mount Zion, but came to be called by the same name. In fact, the term Zion came to be applied poetically to the Holy City as a whole.

"Solomon reigned in Jerusalem over all Israel forty years." (1 Kings 11:42 NIV) However, as he grew older, Solomon began catering to the desires of his many foreign wives to worship the gods of their native lands. He had married "many foreign women besides Pharaoh's daughter—Moabites, Ammonites, Edomites, Sidonians and Hittites. They were from nations about which the LORD had told the Israelites, 'You must not intermarry with them, because they will surely turn your hearts after their gods.'" (1 Kings 11:1-2 NIV)

Solomon's unfaithfulness went so far that "He followed Ashtoreth the goddess of the Sidonians, and Molech the detestable god of the Ammonites. . . . On a hill east of Jerusalem, Solomon built a high place for Chemosh the detestable god of Moab, and for Molech the detestable god of the Ammonites. He did the same for all his foreign wives, who burned incense and offered sacrifices to their gods." (1 Kings 11:5-8 NIV) As a result, God announced that he would rip most of the kingdom away from Solomon and his royal descendents.

Jeroboam son of Nebat of the Israelite tribe of Ephraim began a rebellion against Solomon and, after the king died and his son Rehoboam began to rule in his place, Jeroboam succeeded in getting most of the twelve tribes to break away and make him king over them. So, while Solomon's son Rehoboam and his successors continued to rule over the tribe of Judah in Jerusalem, Jeroboam and his successors ruled over a northern kingdom of Israel from the city of Samaria.

The two kingdoms warred against each other much of the time, Jews fighting Jews in bitter rivalry. The Bible books of 1 Kings and 2 Kings relate the parallel histories of the two Jewish realms.

Eventually the empire of Assyria invaded the northern kingdom, and carried off its Jewish population as captives. But kings in the lineage of David continued to rule in Jerusalem over the tiny kingdom of Judah.

However, the Jews in the southern kingdom followed the pattern of the northern kingdom and repeatedly broke God's covenant. There were "things used to worship Baal, Asherah, and the stars" in the temple at Jerusalem, and "men that the kings of Judah had appointed to offer sacrifices to Baal and to the sun, moon, and stars," as well as a "sacred pole for Asherah" in the temple, and "male prostitutes lived next to the temple" to carry out the homosexual acts that were part of such pagan worship rites. (2 Chronicles 34.4-7 Contemporary English Version)

God is not one to be mocked. As he had said he would a long time earlier in the law of Moses, God punished the Jews for such unfaithfulness. He used the Babylonian empire to carry out his sentence against Israel. First Judah was occupied and subjugated by emperor Nebuchadnezzar. Then, when king Zedekiah rebelled against the Babylonians, they burned Jerusalem and carried off its population as captives.

The Hebrew prophet Daniel prophesied in the royal palace of the Babylonian monarch. Later, when the Medo-Persian empire defeated Babylon, he prophesied under Cyrus the king of Persia and Darius the Mede. Finally, after a seventy year period of captivity foretold by the prophet Jeremiah, the Jews were allowed to return and rebuild Jerusalem with the blessing of the new world power. "In the first year of Cyrus king of Persia, in order to fulfill the word of the LORD spoken by Jeremiah, the LORD moved the heart of Cyrus king of Persia to make a proclamation throughout his realm and to put it in writing: 'This is what Cyrus king of Persia says: "The LORD, the God of heaven, has given me all the kingdoms of the earth and he has appointed me to build a temple for him at Jerusalem in Judah. Anyone of his people among you—may the LORD his God be with him, and let him go up."'" (2 Chron. 36:22-23 NIV)

The restoration of the Jews to the Promised Land at the end of their Babylonian captivity gives us some insight into how God would eventually restore the Jewish people in modern times as we approach the period characterized in the Bible as the final days of this world. How did Israel manage to return to Jerusalem? Observers may not have recognized it as the hand of God. Instead, it may have appeared to be political maneuvering on the part of the world powers of the day. In fact, the Bible records those very maneuverings in considerable detail. But, it also makes it clear that these things took place as the hand of God moved behind the scenes to bring about the outcome that he had foretold through his prophets.

People who say today that the events involving Israel and Palestine are merely political events without God's intervention would probably have said the same thing back then. But God caused the seventy year captivity of the Jewish people to end precisely when he predicted that it would. And this holds great lessons for us today. Although our eyes behold only the visible maneuverings of Israeli political parties and Palestinian factions, the influence of American presidents and United Nations Secretaries General, and the climate of world opinion, behind it all the hand of God is moving again to bring about the outcome foretold in the Bible.

But, keeping that most important lesson in mind, let's return to the story of Jerusalem. The Medo-Persian empire dominated the Middle East until it fell before the armies of Alexander the Great. After Alexander's death, his empire broke into four parts. Eventually the Roman empire came to control the territory that had formerly made up the kingdoms of Israel and Judah. Thus it was that Jerusalem was occupied by Roman soldiers at the time of Christ.

Jesus preached there, and he was put on trial there before Roman governor Pontius Pilate and before the Jewish Sanhedrin court. He was executed outside the city as the Scriptures about the Messiah foretold.

Shortly before his death Jesus visited the temple in Jerusalem with some of his disciples, and they pointed out to him the impressive buildings. He replied, "Do you see all these things? I tell you the truth, not one stone here will be left on another; every one will be thrown down." So, later they asked him privately, "Tell us when will this happen, and what will be the sign of your coming and of the end of the age?" (Matt. 24:2-3 NIV) The disciples actually asked Jesus a three-part question: about the destruction of the temple, about his coming, and about the end of the world, or the end of the age. In his response Jesus added to his prediction of the destruction of the temple these words about the city itself: "Jerusalem will be trampled on by the Gentiles until the times of the Gentiles are fulfilled." (Luke 21:24 NIV)

A few decades after Jesus' crucifixion, Jewish zealots rebelled against the Roman empire. They set Jerusalem free from Roman occupation. However, Roman armies returned and laid siege to the city. Again, there were political and military maneuverings, but the outcome was as Jesus had said: the Roman armies destroyed Jerusalem, tore down the temple, and left not so much as one stone upon another stone.

It was at this point that the Romans carried off the remaining Jews captive and scattered them throughout the Roman empire. This was in fulfillment of the words God gave Moses to record: "But it shall come about, if you do not obey the LORD your God . . . the LORD will scatter you among all peoples, from one end of the earth to the other end of the earth." (Deut. 28:15, 64 NASB)

The Romans re-took and destroyed Jerusalem in 70 A.D. The Roman empire continued to control Jerusalem and its environs until the empire itself began to fall apart. Then the eastern or Byzantine empire ruled from Constantinople. Centuries passed. The city's site was occupied by nomadic Arab tribesmen. Then Mohammed founded a new religion. The Islamic holy war of conquest began and spread across the Middle East and North Africa. Jerusalem fell to the Muslims in the year 638 A.D., six years after Mohammed's death.

During the first hundred years of Muslim control over Jerusalem, ruling Caliphs built two new structures on the mount formerly occupied by the Jewish temple: first, the Dome of the Rock, and then the al-Aqsa mosque. Jerusalem was already a holy city for Muslims, because they held Jesus to be a prophet and recognized some of the Hebrew prophets, and because their Koran says that the Jews "were required to preserve the Book of ALLAH" and that "they were guardians over it." (5: 45) Now the construction of these two buildings further cemented Jerusalem's status as a holy city for Islam.

Events moved slowly in those days, but the Islamic occupation of Jerusalem eventually brought a reaction from the nations that called themselves Christian. Armies of Crusaders reached Jerusalem and took the city in 1099 A.D. But it was difficult for Europeans to control land in the Middle East during the dark ages, and Crusader influence lasted a scant hundred and fifty years or so.

Egyptian influence then prevailed over the city for the most part until the early 1500s, when the Ottoman Turks took control. Napoleon hoped to extend his influence that far after capturing Egypt, but he failed. The Ottoman Turks held onto Jerusalem until their alliance with the Kaiser's Germany in the First World War led to defeat.

British forces under General Allenby marched into the holy city in 1917. The League of Nations legitimized British occupation through an official Mandate. The Balfour Declaration (quoted in another chapter of this book) spelled out Britain's intention to restore a Jewish state in the region. But, when Britain dragged its feet and years passed, Jewish radicals began using force to persuade the British to leave.

In 1947, United Nations General Assembly Resolution 181 called for a division of the land between Jews and Arabs, between two new states of Israel and Jordan, with Jerusalem under U.N. control and administration. Finally, in 1948 as British forces withdrew and the State of Israel was proclaimed, the surrounding Arab nations attacked. Their aim was to destroy Israel and to drive the Jews into the sea. That war ended in 1949 with an agreement dividing Jerusalem between Israel and Jordan.

A few years later, during the Six-Day War, Jewish control over Jerusalem was expanded on June 7, 1967, when the Old City was captured. Then, in 1980, Israel annexed East Jerusalem and declared the united city of Jerusalem to be its capital.

During the 1990's the peace process between Israel and the Palestinians appeared to be moving forward and was about to result in an independent Palestinian state in part of the territory controlled by Israel. Virtually everything had been agreed upon, except the status of Jerusalem. When the topic came up, however, it resulted in the collapse of the peace process and the resumption of the Palestinian uprising.

Under the administration of President George W. Bush the United States government abandoned its long-standing policy of outward neutrality between Israel and the Palestinians. With tacit American support Israel used its military to resolve the conflict in its favor.

And this brings us to the present situation, with Jerusalem now a problem for the whole world, and with the nations of the world working together to impose a solution. "Jerusalem will be a heavy stone burdening the world," as the ancient Hebrew prophet Zechariah said, and, "All the nations of the earth unite in an attempt" to impose their solution. (Zech. 12:3 The Living Bible)

As detailed in other chapters of this book, there are United Nations resolutions calling for the state of Israel to abandon its claim to Jerusalem as its eternal capital, and to withdraw from at least part of the city. Other U.N. resolutions call for all of Jerusalem to be an international city under direct United Nations control. There are strong political currents in the international community for these resolutions to be enforced.

What will happen? Eventually the nations of the world, 'united' as Zechariah foretold, will move to enforce their will. But, they will find themselves up against the will of God. The battle of Armageddon will be fought, and God will prevail.

What, then will be the future of Jerusalem? God's intention is for it to be restored as the center for his worship for the whole world: "At that time they will call Jerusalem The Throne of the LORD, and all nations will gather in Jerusalem to honor the name of the LORD. No longer will they follow the stubbornness of their evil hearts." (Jeremiah 3:17 NIV) The words of Jeremiah 31:35-40 (NIV) make very plain what lies ahead for the holy city Jerusalem:

"This is what the LORD says, he who appoints the sun to shine by day, who decrees the moon and stars to shine by night, who stirs up the sea so that its waves roar—the LORD Almighty is his name: 'Only if these decrees vanish from my sight,' declares the LORD, 'will the descendants of Israel ever cease to be a nation before me.' This is what the LORD says: 'Only if the heavens above can be

measured and the foundations of the earth below be searched out will I reject all the descendants of Israel because of all they have done,' declares the LORD. 'The days are coming,' declares the LORD, 'when this city will be rebuilt for me from the Tower of Hananel to the Corner Gate. The measuring line will stretch from there straight to the hill of Gareb and then turn to Goah. The whole valley where dead bodies and ashes are thrown, and all the terraces out to the Kidron Valley on the east as far as the corner of the Horse Gate, will be holy to the LORD. The city will never again be uprooted or demolished."

According to the second Psalm, God's anointed Messiah will rule the world from Mount Zion in Jerusalem:

"Why do the nations conspire and the peoples plot in vain?
The kings of the earth take their stand
and the rulers gather together against the LORD
and against his Anointed One.
'Let us break their chains,' they say, 'and throw off their fetters.'
The One enthroned in heaven laughs; the LORD scoffs at them.
Then he rebukes them in his anger and terrifies them in his wrath, saying,
'I have installed my King on Zion, my holy hill.'
I will proclaim the decree of the LORD :
He said to me, 'You are my Son; today I have become your Father.
Ask of me, and I will make the nations your inheritance, the ends of the earth your possession.
You will rule them with an iron scepter; you will dash them to pieces like pottery.'
Therefore, you kings, be wise;
be warned, you rulers of the earth. Serve the LORD with fear
and rejoice with trembling. Kiss the Son, lest he be angry
and you be destroyed in your way, for his wrath can flare up in a moment. Blessed are all who take refuge in him."

—Psalm 2 NIV

Promised Messiah

George Frideric Handel's centuries-old musical masterpiece titled *Messiah* begins with Isaiah's prophecy of a gospel message, or message of good news, coming to Jerusalem:

"Comfort ye, comfort ye my people, saith your God. Speak ye comfortably to Jerusalem, and cry unto her, that her warfare is accomplished, that her iniquity is pardoned. . . . O thou that tellest good tidings to Zion, get thee up into the high mountain; O thou that tellest good tidings to Jerusalem, lift up thy voice with strength; lift it up, and be not afraid; say unto the cities of Judah, Behold your God!"

—Isaiah 40:1-2, 9 KJV

And Handel concludes his masterpiece with words from the Apostle John's Apocalypse depicting the Messiah as a sacrificial lamb, raised from the dead to glory in heaven:

"Worthy is the Lamb that was slain to receive power, and riches, and wisdom, and strength, and honour, and glory, and blessing. . . . Blessing, and honour, glory and power, be unto Him that sitteth upon the throne, and unto the Lamb for ever and ever. . . . Amen."

—Revelation 5:12-14 KJV

The rest of the lyrics of Handel's masterpiece are likewise made up entirely of Scripture, set to music to tell the story of God's Messiah or Christ beautifully and powerfully. But Handel's *Messiah* can be best appreciated by those who are familiar with the whole story found in the Bible itself.

There is some overlapping between the story of the Messiah and the story of the Promised Seed, because they both end up being fulfilled by the same person, Jesus Christ. As noted in the chapter of this book titled "Promised Seed," the New Testament documents the genealogy of Jesus' lineage back to the royal house of King David, both through his mother Mary and through his adoptive father Joseph. (Matt. 1:1-17 and Luke 3:23-38). This is a critical factor in identifying him as the fulfillment of the promise.

That is because our English word Messiah comes from a Hebrew word of similar pronunciation which means "anointed one." The word Christ comes from a Greek word for "anointed one." Both terms originally referred to a king chosen by God, because the first Israelite kings were designated as rulers when God's prophet anointed them by ceremonially pouring oil over their heads. The promised Messiah would, himself, be a future king, one descended from the ancient kings of Israel.

For a few hundred years after their exodus from Egypt, right up until around 1000 B.C., the Jews lived in the Promised Land under a loose, decentralized form of tribal government. They had no king. Each tribe had its elders, and these handled any judicial cases that could not be cared for by local village elders and heads of families. Whenever the twelve tribes needed to take action on some matter that transcended tribal lines—such as national defense in the face of invading armies—God would raise up a "judge" as an ad hoc ruler.

The Bible book titled "Judges" contains the record of Jewish history during this period. Moses' commander general and eventual successor Joshua was the first judge. Gideon, Deborah and Samson are other names that stand out among the judges. But, eventually the people began to complain that they wanted a king to rule over them, like the nations round about.

The prophet Samuel then received instructions from God to anoint Israel's first king. He was sent to the family of "Kish, the son of Abiel, the son of Zeror, the son of Bechorath, the son of Aphiah, a Benjamite, a mighty man of power." (1 Samuel 9:1 KJV) When the Lord revealed to Samuel that his choice was Kish's son Saul, "Then Samuel took a flask of oil and poured it on Saul's head and kissed him, saying, 'Has not the LORD anointed you leader over his inheritance?'" (1 Samuel 10:1 NIV)

However, Saul later proved unfaithful, and God had Samuel anoint David, son of Jesse, to succeed him. Sheep herder Jesse brought seven of his sons before the prophet, one by one, but left the youngest to watch the sheep. Yet it turned out to be this one that God had chosen. "The LORD said, 'Arise, anoint him; for this is he.' Then Samuel took the horn of oil, and anointed him in the midst of his brothers; and the Spirit of the LORD came mightily upon David from that day forward. . . . Now the Spirit of the LORD departed from Saul." (1 Samuel 16:12-14 RSV) So David, too, was a Messiah or anointed one. Kings in David's line continued to rule in Jerusalem for generations, some of them faithful to God, but others unfaithful as Saul had been.

Throughout that period inspired prophets pointed forward to a time when the ultimate Messiah would come, a Messiah who would not need a successor, because he would live forever and his rulership would last forever. First, though, he would be killed, and would rise again, immortal, and would eventually take power to rule the whole world in righteousness, on into eternity.

A hint of the coming Messiah was provided by the prophet Nathan who gave this divine revelation to David:

"'The LORD declares to you that the LORD himself will establish a house for you: When your days are over and you rest with your fathers, I will raise up your offspring to succeed you, who will come

from your own body, and I will establish his kingdom. He is the one who will build a house for my Name, and I will establish the throne of his kingdom forever. I will be his father, and he will be my son. When he does wrong, I will punish him with the rod of men, with floggings inflicted by men. But my love will never be taken away from him, as I took it away from Saul, whom I removed from before you. Your house and your kingdom will endure forever before me; your throne will be established forever.'"

—2 Sam. 7:11-16 NIV

David's son Solomon succeeded his father and built the temple in Jerusalem. But God's promise of someone from the house of David ruling "forever" was not fulfilled in Solomon, nor was God's reference to a future king who would be "my son." Kings from the house of David ruled in Jerusalem for nearly four hundred years, but around 600 B.C. that rule was interrupted when the neo-Babylonian empire took the city and destroyed the temple. From that point onward faithful Jews looked to God to send them a son of David who would restore the kingdom in Jerusalem. They began hoping for the promised Messiah.

Daniel wrote:

"Know therefore and understand, that from the going forth of the commandment to restore and to build Jerusalem unto the Messiah the Prince shall be seven weeks, and threescore and two weeks: the street shall be built again, and the wall, even in troublous times. And after threescore and two weeks shall Messiah be cut off, but not for himself: and the people of the prince that shall come shall destroy the city and the sanctuary; and the end thereof shall be with a flood, and unto the end of the war desolations are determined."

—Daniel 9:25-26 KJV

The "seven weeks, and threescore and two weeks" (7 + 60 +2 = 69) are widely understood as weeks of years—seven years each, rather than seven days—with "each day for a year" (Num. 14:34, Ezek. 4:6 KJV) So, the 69 x 7 = 483 years are understood as the time interval from the command to restore and rebuild Jerusalem during the reign of Persian King Artaxerxes, as related in the second chapter of Nehemiah, until Christ appeared 483 years later.

Isaiah foretold many additional details about this promised Messiah:

He would be born of a Virgin:

"Therefore the LORD himself shall give you a sign; Behold, a virgin shall conceive, and bear a son, and shall call his name Immanuel."

His ministry would be largely in Galilee:

"Nevertheless, there will be no more gloom for those who were in distress. In the past he humbled the land of Zebulun and the land of Naphtali, but in the future he will honor Galilee of the Gentiles, by the way of the sea, along the Jordan— The people walking in darkness have seen a great light; on those living in the land of the shadow of death a light has dawned."

—Isaiah 9:1-2 NIV

He would become earth's ruler forever:

"For unto us a child is born, unto us a son is given: and the government shall be upon his shoulder: and his name shall be called Wonderful, Counsellor, The mighty God, The everlasting Father, The Prince of Peace. Of the increase of his government and peace there shall be no end, upon the throne of David, and upon his kingdom, to order it, and to establish it with judgment and with justice from henceforth even for ever. The zeal of the LORD of hosts will perform this."

—Isaiah 9:6-7 KJV

He would be descended from Jesse, king David's father:

"And there shall come forth a rod out of the stem of Jesse, and a Branch shall grow out of his roots: And the spirit of the LORD shall rest upon him, the spirit of wisdom and understanding, the spirit of counsel and might, the spirit of knowledge and of the fear of the LORD."

—Isaiah 11:1-2 KJV

People from non-Jewish nations would turn to him and glorify him:

"And in that day there shall be a root of Jesse, which shall stand for an ensign of the people; to it shall the Gentiles seek: and his rest shall be glorious."

—Isaiah 11:10 KJV

Meek and gentle, his teachings would bring hope and the light of God's law to the non-Jewish nations:

"Behold my servant, whom I uphold; mine elect, in whom my soul delighteth; I have put my spirit upon him: he shall bring forth judgment to the Gentiles. He shall not cry, nor lift up, nor cause his voice to be heard in the street. A bruised reed shall he not break, and the smoking flax shall he not quench: he shall bring forth judgment unto truth. He shall not fail nor be discouraged, till he have set judgment in the earth: and the isles shall wait for his law. . . . I the LORD have called thee in righteousness, and will hold thine hand, and will keep thee, and give thee for a covenant of the people, for a light of the Gentiles; To open the blind eyes, to bring out the prisoners from the prison, and them that sit in darkness out of the prison house."

—Isaiah 42:1-7 KJV

He would be rejected by the Jewish people:

"For he shall grow up before him as a tender plant, and as a root out of a dry ground: he hath no form nor comeliness; and when we shall see him, there is no beauty that we should desire him. He is despised and rejected of men; a man of sorrows, and acquainted with grief: and we hid as it were our faces from him; he was despised, and we esteemed him not."

—Isaiah 53:2-3 KJV

He would be scourged and, by God's arrangement, would take the sins of mankind upon himself:

"Surely he hath borne our griefs, and carried our sorrows: yet we did esteem him stricken, smitten of God, and afflicted. But he was wounded for our transgressions, he was bruised for our iniquities: the chastisement of our peace was upon him; and with his stripes we are healed. All we like sheep have gone astray; we have turned every one to his own way; and the LORD hath laid on him the iniquity of us all."

—Isaiah 53:4-6 KJV

He would be put to death for the sins of mankind, like a sacrificial lamb:

"He was oppressed, and he was afflicted, yet he opened not his mouth: he is brought as a lamb to the slaughter, and as a sheep before her shearers is dumb, so he openeth not his mouth. He was taken from prison and from judgment: and who shall declare his generation? for he was cut off out of the land of the living: for the transgression of my people was he stricken."

—Isaiah 53:7-8 KJV

He would be buried in a rich man's grave:

"And he made his grave with the wicked, and with the rich in his death; because he had done no violence, neither [was any] deceit in his mouth."

His sacrificial death would free others from their sins:

"Yet it pleased the LORD to bruise him; he hath put his to grief: when thou shalt make his soul an offering for sin . . . the pleasure of the LORD shall prosper in his hand. He shall see of the travail of his soul, and shall be satisfied: by his knowledge shall my righteous servant justify many; for he shall bear their iniquities. . . . he hath poured out his soul unto death: and he was numbered with the transgressors; and he bare the sin of many, and made intercession for the transgressors."

—Isaiah 53:10-12 KJV

Other biblical prophets were similarly inspired to add further details about the promised Messiah:

He would be born in Bethlehem, and would be struck on the face:

"They will strike Israel's ruler on the cheek with a rod. But you, Bethlehem Ephrathah, though you are small among the clans of Judah, out of you will come for me one who will be ruler over Israel, whose origins are from of old, from ancient times."

—Micah 5:1-2 NIV

He would be nailed up to die, with the executioners dividing his clothing:

"the assembly of the wicked have inclosed me: they pierced my hands and my feet. I may tell all my bones: they look and stare upon me. They part my garments among them, and cast lots upon my vesture."

—Psalm 22:16-18 KJV

Besides foretelling Jerusalem's role in the Bible's end times scenario, the prophet Zechariah also foretold several additional details concerning the Messiah's life and death:

He would be humble and would present himself to Jerusalem by arriving seated on a donkey:

"Rejoice greatly, O daughter of Zion; shout, O daughter of Jerusalem: behold, thy King cometh unto thee: he is just, and having salvation; lowly, and riding upon an ass, and upon a colt the foal of an ass."

—Zechariah 9:9 KJV

He would be betrayed for thirty pieces of silver, which would be thrown into the temple and used to buy the potter's field:

"And I said unto them, If ye think good, give me my price; and if not, forbear. So they weighed for my price thirty pieces of silver. And the LORD said unto me, Cast it unto the potter: a goodly price that I was prised at of them. And I took the thirty pieces of silver, and cast them to the potter in the house of the LORD."

—Zechariah 11:12-13 KJV

So, to sum up these Old Testament prophecies, the promised Messiah would be descended from the house of David, yet would somehow also be the son of God. He would be born in Bethlehem, the child of a virgin, would preach in Galillee, would arrive in Jerusalem seated on a donkey, but would be rejected, beaten, stripped, and nailed up to die like a criminal. His betrayer would be paid thirty pieces of silver. He would rise again, immortal, and would be accepted and glorified by non-Jewish peoples around the world.

Jesus of Nazareth fit every detail of the prophetic description, but only a small minority of the Jewish people accepted him as their promised Messiah. These Jews who rejoiced at the "gospel," or message of good news, formed the nucleus of congregations that met together to share encouragement. As predicted, Gentiles too accepted the message, and they soon outnumbered the Messianic Jewish believers. Unable to read Hebrew, most of these Gentile believers heard or read the message in their contemporary universal Greek language and referred to themselves as followers of "Christ." It was in such a mixed congregation of Jewish and Gentile converts in ancient Antioch that the disciples were first called "Christians." (Acts 11:26)

Jesus had instructed his followers to "go and make disciples of all nations." (Matt. 28:19 NIV) And he had told them that "this gospel of the kingdom will be preached in the whole world as a testimony to all nations, and then the end will come." (Matt. 24:14 NIV)

An Islamic Antichrist

'If you become a Christian, we will kill you.' That is what Islam teaches more than a billion of its followers worldwide.

Sometimes the death sentence is imposed by governments. Other times the execution is carried out by neighborhood thugs. But it is the official position of Islamic authorities that Muslim converts to Christianity must be killed according to Islamic law. And it is a threat that does not have to be carried out very often to accomplish its intended result—to intimidate Muslims and prevent them from choosing to follow Jesus.

A popular notion among many American churchgoers today is that a future Antichrist will arise who will make it punishable by death if anyone declares himself to be a follower of Jesus. But that is already the case in much of the world where Islam holds sway. Could Islam itself be the expected Antichrist? You may be surprised to learn that such notable Bible commentators as Martin Luther and John Calvin answered Yes.

Unlike the major religions of the world that arose independently, Islam arose as a response to Christianity—a hostile response. And Islam has remained hostile to Christians and to Jews throughout its existence. However, that hostility has greatly increased since the restoration of the state of Israel in 1948 and Jewish control over Jerusalem in 1967.

Does the Bible speak prophetically of the rise of Islam? Yes, it does—according to such respected students of the Bible as Martin Luther, John Calvin, Sir Isaac Newton and Jonathan Edwards. But before looking at what these men wrote, let's look at a bit of history and a bit of Scripture. Then it will be easier to see whether Islam fits the pattern that Luther, Calvin and Newton pointed to in the Bible.

The founders of Hinduism and Buddhism knew nothing of the Gospel of Jesus Christ, but the founders of the Islamic religion were already familiar with the Christian Gospel message, and they rejected it—denying that Jesus is the Son of God.

In fact, one of the chief tenets of Islam—adopted to repudiate the teachings of Christianity—is the assertion that God has no son.

Interestingly, that is exactly how the Bible describes the "Antichrist." There are only three passages in the Bible that use the term "Antichrist," and they are all found in the letters of the Apostle John. This is what he wrote:

"you have heard that the antichrist is coming, even now many antichrists have come. . . . They went out from us, but they did not really belong to us. . . . Who is the liar? It is the man who denies that Jesus is the Christ. Such a man is the antichrist—he denies the Father and the Son. . . . I am writing these things to you about those who are trying to lead you astray."

— 1 John 2:18-26 NIV

"Dear friends, do not believe every spirit, but test the spirits to see whether they are from God, because many false prophets have gone out into the world. This is how you can recognize the Spirit of God: Every spirit that acknowledges that Jesus Christ has come in the flesh is from God, but every spirit that does not acknowledge Jesus is not from God. This is the spirit of the antichrist, which you have heard is coming and even now is already in the world."

— 1 John 4:1-3 NIV

"Many deceivers, who do not acknowledge Jesus Christ as coming in the flesh, have gone out into the world. Any such person is the deceiver and the antichrist."

— 2 John 7 NIV

Do any of those descriptions fit Islam?

The Muslim holy book, the Koran, makes a number of references to Jesus. It calls him "Isa, the son of Marium" (Jesus, the son of Mary). The Koran admonishes Mohammed's followers to believe in the revelation given by God "to Abraham, Ishmael, Isaac, Jacob, and the Tribes, and that given to Moses and Jesus." (2:136) It says that Jesus was sent by God, empowered to do miracles and strengthened through the Holy Spirit. (2:87, 253) It acknowledges that he healed lepers, gave sight to the blind and raised the dead by the power of God. (5:110) It affirms that Jesus was born of a virgin, and that he was taken up to God's presence. (19:20; 4:157-158)

But then Islam goes on to deny that Jesus is the only-begotten Son of God. So, it is actually an apostasy from Christianity, and therefore fits John's description of "antichrists" who "went out from among us" and deny "the Father and the Son."

Moreover, Islam forbids its subjects from becoming followers of Jesus—from accepting him as their Lord and Savior. Those who do embrace Christ face intense persecution, prison and even death. Their stories seldom become headlines in Western news media, but there are currently a number of Muslim converts to Christianity on death row in strict Muslim countries, convicted in court of such offenses as "apostasy," "leaving Islam," or "insulting the Prophet Mohammed." And there are many others who have been murdered by relatives or neighbors for the same reasons, with Muslim police and authorities turning a blind eye.

Consider, too, another Bible passage that commentators often apply to the Antichrist:

"Who opposeth and exalteth himself above all that is called God, or that is worshipped; so that he as God sitteth in the temple of God, shewing himself that he is God."

—2 Thessalonians 2:4 KJV

The New International Version puts it this way:

"He will oppose and will exalt himself over everything that is called God or is worshiped, so that he sets himself up in God's temple, proclaiming himself to be God."

—2 Thessalonians 2:4 NIV

Islam opposes all other forms of worship, but what about God's temple in Jerusalem? Has Islam set itself up there, in God's place? God's temple in Jerusalem was destroyed by Roman armies almost two thousand years ago. Some students of the Bible expect a future Antichrist to build another temple there, to fulfill the prophecy of 2 Thessalonians 2:4. But Islam has already built a temple there. Might the prophecy be fulfilled by the structures sitting in God's place on Temple Mount since shortly after the Islamic conquest?

To fulfill the prophecy, is it necessary for someone or some group to say the words "I am God"? Or is sitting in God's place equivalent to declaring oneself to be God?

"The entire top of the hill where the Temple is built is holy," according to Ezekiel 43:12 (LB). An Islamic temple called the Dome of the Rock sits there today, and it bears an inscription saying it was built by "the servant of God Abd al-Malik Ibn Marwan, emir of the faithful, in the year seventy-two." (The year 72 in the Muslim calendar is 691-692 A.D.) Adjacent to it sits the Al Aqsa Mosque which was built around the same time, and has been rebuilt a number of times over the centuries.

"The entire top of the hill where the Temple is built is holy."

—Ezekiel 43:12 LB

". . . he takes his seat in the temple of God, displaying himself as being God."

—2 Thessalonians 2:4 NASB

Who is sitting in God's place on Temple Mount?

Dome of the Rock

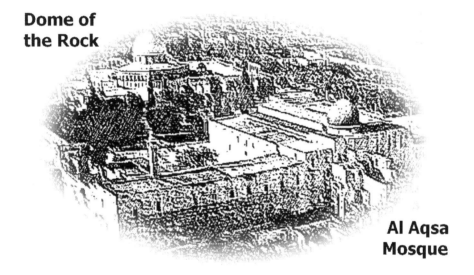

Al Aqsa Mosque

". . . he sits as God in the temple of God, setting himself up as God."

—2 Thessalonians 2:4 WEB

"The entire top of the mountain where the Temple is built is holy."

—Ezekiel 43:12 NLT

Do the owners of these structures that sit in God's place on Temple Mount fit the biblical description of an Antichrist? Consider what the Arabic inscriptions on the walls of the Dome of the Rock say about Jesus Christ. Are they the sort of statements we would expect of an Antichrist? These inscriptions repeatedly deny that Jesus is the Son of God. They say:

> "Oh God, bless Your Messenger and Your servant Jesus son of Mary. Peace be on him the day he was born, and the day he dies, and the day he shall be raised alive!"

> "God is only One God. Far be it removed from His transcendent majesty that He should have a son."

> "The Messiah, Jesus son of Mary, was only a Messenger of God, and His Word which He conveyed unto Mary, and a spirit from Him."

> "Such was Jesus, son of Mary... It befitteth not God that He should take unto Himself a son."

> "Praise be to God, Who hath not taken unto Himself a son."

Notice how closely these inscriptions on the walls of the Dome of the Rock fit the Apostle John's definition of an Antichrist as "the man who denies that Jesus is the Christ. Such a man is the antichrist—he denies the Father and the Son. No one who denies the Son has the Father." (1 John 2:22-23) So, could this Dome of the Rock, which sits in God's place on Temple Mount, be Antichrist's temple? Before dismissing the possibility, consider that the Islamic occupier of Temple Mount was also identified as Antichrist in the words of both John Calvin and Martin Luther.

Calvin and Luther lived in an era when people who chose to read the Bible and follow Jesus were being put to death by enemies of biblical Christianity. The pope of Rome was executing people who wanted to read and follow the Bible, and Islamic armies were conquering Christian lands and leading their inhabitants to renounce belief in Christ. Luther and Calvin identified both of those enemies as the Antichrist.

For centuries the Roman Catholic papacy had been using the Inquisition to stop ordinary people from reading the Bible in their own language. The papacy was burning Bible-readers at the stake as "heretics." Prominent among these were Czech Bible translator John Hus, executed in 1415, and English Bible translator William Tyndale, executed in 1536—but there were thousands of others killed by the Inquisition and other papal authorities. And, during the same time period, the armies of Islam were threatening Christendom from the east and from the west—Moors in Spain until the late 1400's and Ottoman Turks invading eastern Europe and even besieging Vienna, Austria, in 1529.

So, Martin Luther and John Calvin spoke of Antichrist as having two legs or two horns: one leg the papacy and the other Islam, or one horn the papacy and the other Islam.

Calvin saw the Pope and "Mahomet" as "the two horns of the Antichrist." He declared, "Lyke as Mahomet saith ty his Alcoran is ye soveraine wisdome, so saith the Pope of his owne decrees: For they be the two hornes of Antichrist." (*The Sermons of M. John Calvin upon the Fifth Booke of Moses called Deuteronomie*, translated by Arthur Golding, first published in London, 1583, from a facsimile reprint by Banner of Truth Trust, 1987.) Or, to put that archaic English into modern speech, "Like as Mohammed says that his Koran is the sovereign wisdom, so says the Pope of his own decrees: For they are the two horns of Antichrist."

Calvin also wrote, "Paul, however, does not speak of one individual, but of a kingdom, that was to be taken possession of by Satan, that he might set up a seat of abomination in the midst of God's temple—which we see accomplished in Popery. The revolt, it is true, has spread more widely, for Mahomet, as he was an apostate, turned away the Turks, his followers, from Christ." (Calvin's *Commentary on Philippians, Colossians, and Thessalonians*)

If Calvin saw the papacy and Islam as the two "horns" of the Antichrist, Martin Luther saw them as the two "legs" of the same Antichrist. (Luther's Works, Weimer ed., 53, 394f.) Luther added, "the Pope is the spirit of antichrist, and the Turk is the flesh of antichrist. They help each other in their murderous work. The latter slaughters bodily by the sword; and the former spiritually by doctrine." (Luther's *Tischreden*, Weimer ed., 1, No. 330)

So, in their writings quoted above, both John Calvin and Martin Luther interpreted Scripture about the Antichrist as finding fulfillment in Islam.

Sir Isaac Newton saw a similar fulfillment in regard to the Islamic conquest of the Middle East and North Africa. But before looking at what Newton wrote, a brief history and geography lesson will help to put it in perspective.

The disciples of Jesus obeyed Christ's command to "go and make disciples of all nations" (Matt. 28:19 NIV), and by the year 600 A.D. Christianity was the prevailing religion from the British Isles across Europe and Eurasia to the Black Sea, south to the Tigris and Euphrates Rivers, farther south to the Nile River in Egypt, and across North Africa to the straits of Gibraltar. Besides the southern European countries, the lands we know today as Morocco, Tunisia, Algeria, Libya, Egypt, Jordan, Syria, Turkey and Iraq were largely Christian by the seventh century A.D. Then came the Islamic conquest of the mid-to-late 600's and early 700's. Today those same countries of North Africa and the Middle East are almost exclusively Muslim.

During the centuries after the Muslim armies swept across the region there were periods of intense pressure on the Christian inhabitants to convert to Islam, interspersed with other periods of hostile toleration of Christianity. Even during the best of times believers in Jesus were relegated to second-class citizenship, and were burdened with extra taxation for not being Muslims.

The Bible book of Acts and the letters of the Apostle Paul focus largely on cities in modern-day Turkey—Lystra, Iconium, Derbe, Galatia, Ephesus, Colossae. Tradition has it that the Christian church in Antioch, Turkey, near the border with Syria, was founded by the Apostle Peter in the year 37 A.D. And it was there that the term "Christians" was first used: "The disciples were called Christians first at Antioch." (Acts 11:26 NIV) The seven churches named in the opening chapters of the Bible book of Revelation were all located in Turkey. And the Apostle Paul's letters to the churches of the Galatians, Ephesians and Colossians were written to churches in Turkey. Today Turkey is 99.8% Muslim. It is illegal for Christians to preach the Gospel to Muslims, and Muslims who choose to follow Jesus may face violence and even death.

According to tradition the Christian Gospel was brought to Iraq by two of the original Twelve Apostles—Thomas and Thaddeus. And Iraq was largely Christian for centuries prior to the Islamic invasion. Modern Iraq is now 97% Muslim. Christians are forbidden to preach the Gospel to the Islamic majority, and Muslims who convert to Christianity may be killed.

Egypt was predominantly Christian for centuries prior to the Muslim invasion. Today Egypt is 90% Muslim, with only 10% of Egyptians professing Christianity.

Syria, 90% Muslim today, had been largely Christian for centuries. Today only about 10% of Syrians profess Christianity.

Ancient Carthage covered the area known today as Tunisia and Algeria. It was a prominent center for Christian thought before the Islamic conquest, home to early Christian writers Tertullian and St. Augustine. Today Tunisia is 98% Muslim, and Algeria is 99% Muslim.

So, the Islamic conquest of this area was not a conquest of pagan lands. It was a conquest of Christian countries filled with Christian inhabitants.

Was this Muslim conquest foretold in the Bible? Some notable commentators see the spread of Islam in this passage from the book of Daniel:

"And the king shall do according to his will; and he shall exalt himself, and magnify himself above every god, and shall speak marvelous things against the God of gods, and shall prosper till the indignation be accomplished; for that which is determined shall be done. Neither shall he regard the gods of his fathers, nor the desire of women, nor regard any god; for he shall magnify himself above all. . . . And at the time of the end . . . the king of the north shall come . . . like a whirlwind, with chariots, and with horsemen, and with many ships; and he shall enter into the countries, and shall overflow and pass over. He shall enter also into the glorious land, and many countries shall be overthrown: but these shall escape out of his hand, even Edom, and Moab, and the chief of the children of

Ammon. He shall stretch forth his hand also upon the countries: and the land of Egypt shall not escape. But he shall have power over the treasures of gold and of silver, and over all the precious things of Egypt: and the Libyans and the Ethiopians [shall be] at his steps. . . . And he shall plant the tabernacles of his palace between the seas in the glorious holy mountain; yet he shall come to his end, and none shall help him."

—Daniel 11:36-45 KJV

Discussing Daniel 11:36-45, Sir Isaac Newton saw this passage as fulfilled in the Islamic conquest—the lands ruled by the Muslim Turks. He commented to the effect that "these nations compose the Empire of the Turks, and therefore this Empire is here to be understood by the King of the North." (Newton's *The Prophecies of Daniel and The Apocalypse*, p. 189) That Islamic empire and its successors held the Holy Land until the Turks suffered defeat along with their German allies during the First World War and Jerusalem was taken from them by the British in 1917. Considering Muslim hostility toward other religions, along with the oppression of women in Islamic countries, this passage's description of a king rejecting the gods of his fathers and the desire of women could well fit Islam.

Colonial American Congregationalist theologian and missionary Jonathan Edwards (1703-1758), who served also as president of Princeton University, expressed the historic view that prevailed in the Church for hundreds of years that the Islamic sweep over the remnant of the eastern Roman Empire was foretold in Scripture. He summed it up this way:

```
"The Mahometan kingdom is another of mighty power and vast
extent, set up by Satan against the kingdom of Christ. ...
And then the Turks, who were originally different from the
Saracens, became followers of Mahomet, and conquered all
the Eastern empire.  They began their empire about the
year of Christ twelve hundred and ninety-six; began to
invade Europe in the year thirteen hundred; took
Constantinople, and so became masters of all the Eastern
empire, in the year fourteen hundred and fifty-three.  And
thus all the cities and countries where stood those famous
churches of which we read in the New Testament, as
Jerusalem, Antioch, Ephesus, Corinth, &c. now became
subject to the Turks.  These are supposed to be prophesied
of by the horsemen in the 9th chapter of Revelation,
beginning with the 15th verse."
```

(Quoted from Jonathan Edwards' classic, *A History of the Work of Redemption*)

In our modern world political observers in the West have expressed concern over Islamists rising to political power in Muslim countries of the Middle East and North Africa. The world took notice when an Islamic revolution in Iran brought the Ayatollahs to power in the 1970's, and again when the "Arab

Spring" of 2011 toppled secular dictators across the region and gave more political power to Islamic political parties. Dramatic events in Afghanistan and Iraq replaced secular leaders there with others determined to impose Sharia Law based on the Muslim holy book, the Koran.

But, as documented above, Islamic political power is really nothing new. In fact, from its beginnings in the seventh century, Islam was both a religion and a political power. The Constitution of Medina united a few Arab tribes under the prophet Mohammed, and then they conquered Mecca, also on the Arabian Peninsula. During the next few years the lands we know today as Syria, Jordan, Palestine and Iraq fell under Muslim control. Egypt was seized from the Byzantine Empire in the year 645. (Still, historians report that Egypt was majority Christian until around 1400 A.D.)

The prevailing model in countries that are overwhelmingly Muslim, is that Christians are forbidden to preach the Gospel to others. Christian evangelism is outlawed, and conversion to Christianity is illegal. Muslims who decide to follow Jesus may be punished with death—either through the judicial system or by way of extra-judicial mob violence, with authorities turning a blind eye.

There are many Christians who believe that an Antichrist will arise someday during a future tribulation, and that this future Antichrist will make it difficult for believers to practice Christianity. But even today a sizeable portion of the world's population already lives under such circumstances. In April 2012 alone, the news media reported violent Muslim attacks on Christian churches in Kenya, Azerbaijan, Indonesia, Nigeria, Sudan and Tunisia, criminal charges of apostasy or blasphemy being brought against Christians in Algeria, Bangladesh, Egypt, Iran and Pakistan, and Christians being otherwise abused or oppressed by Muslim authorities in Egypt, Iran, Pakistan, Syria, Tunisia and Turkey.

Could anything be more "anti"-Christ than that?

So, might Islam itself be the expected end-times Antichrist?

Daniel's Beasts and the Beasts of Revelation

In popular culture 'the beast of Revelation' is a notorious villain who could easily frighten even viewers of top-grossing horror movies. The *Left Behind* novels portray 'the beast' as a sinister character named Nicolae Capathia, who also happens to be 'the Antichrist.' But what does the Bible really say about 'the beast of Revelation'? Actually, Revelation speaks about a number of beasts—not just one. And they are signs or symbols of governments or organizations, not some individual man or monster.

The Apostle John, who wrote the Revelation or Apocalypse back in the first century, knew that his contemporary readers were already familiar with the much earlier Bible book of Daniel, which spoke of the same sorts of symbolic beasts. And, of course, it was the same God who sent angels and visions to both Daniel and John, and who inspired their writing. So, the beasts of Daniel are key to understanding the beasts of Revelation.

Babylon

"the first was like a lion, and had eagle's wings" – Dan. 7:1 NKJV

Daniel describes four separate beasts

"In the first year of Belshazzar king of Babylon, Daniel had a dream, and visions passed through his mind as he was lying in bed. He wrote down the substance of his dream.

"Daniel said: 'In my vision at night I looked, and there before me were the four winds of heaven churning up the great sea. Four great beasts, each different from the others, came up out of the sea.

"'The first was like a lion, and it had the wings of an eagle. I watched until its wings were torn off and it was lifted from the ground so that it stood on two feet like a human being, and the mind of a human was given to it.

"'And there before me was a second beast, which looked like a bear. It was raised up on one of its sides, and it had three ribs in its mouth between its teeth. It was told, 'Get up and eat your fill of flesh!'

"'After that, I looked, and there before me was another beast, one that looked like a leopard. And on its back it had four wings like those of a bird. This beast had four heads, and it was given authority to rule.

"'After that, in my vision at night I looked, and there before me was a fourth beast—terrifying and frightening and very powerful. It had large iron teeth; it crushed and devoured its victims and trampled underfoot whatever was left. It was different from all the former beasts, and it had ten horns.'"

—Daniel 7:1-7 NIV

Persia

"another beast, a second, like a bear...and it had three ribs in its mouth" – Dan. 7:5 NKJV

Daniel saw in vision a beast "like a lion" with wings, "a second beast, which looked like a bear," "another beast, one that looked like a leopard" and "a fourth beast—terrifying and frightening, and very powerful" with "ten horns." (Dan. 7:2-6 NIV) Naming the very same animals, John saw "a beast" with

"ten horns and seven heads, with ten crowns on its horns, and on each head a blasphemous name. The beast I saw resembled a leopard, but had feet like those of a bear and a mouth like that of a lion."

—Revelation 13:1-2 NIV

106

Greece

"another, like a leopard, which had upon its back four wings of a fowl; the beast had also four heads" – Dan. 7:6 NKJV

An angel gave Daniel "the interpretation of these things," namely that "The four great beasts are four kingdoms that will rise from the earth." (Dan. 7:16-17 NIV) John likewise described the composite beast he saw as having governmental "power" and a "throne and great authority." (Rev. 13:2 NIV)

Daniel's four beasts were four separate successive kingdoms or empires that ruled over much of the earth; the composite beast of Revelation chapter 13 "was given authority over every tribe, people, language and nation." (Rev. 13:7 NIV)

(The reader is encouraged to open the Bible itself and read first-hand what it says about these symbolic beasts and the governments they represent.)

Rome

"a fourth beast, dreadful and terrible, exceedingly strong...and it had ten horns" – Dan. 7:7 NKJV

Bible commentators have long agreed that Daniel's four beasts are the Babylonian, Persian, Greek and Roman empires. Reformer John Calvin was familiar with the works of other scholars and declared in his *Commentaries on the Book of Daniel*, volume 2,

It is clear that the four monarchies are here depicted. But it is not agreed upon among all writers which monarchy is the last, and which the third. With regard to the first, all agree in understanding the vision of the Chaldean Empire, which was joined with the Assyrian, as we saw before. For Nineveh was absorbed by the Chaldeans and Babylonians.

Respected Bible commentator Albert Barnes took a similar position in his *Notes*. Commenting on the beast of Revelation 13:1, he referred back to Daniel's vision and wrote

Thus in Daniel (vii. 2-7) the *lion* is introduced as the symbol of the Babylonian power; the bear, as the symbol of the Medo-Persian; the leopard, as the symbol of the Macedonian; and a nondescript animal, fierce, cruel, and mighty, with two horns, as the symbol of the Roman.

So, while there were differences in the details, most traditional writers agreed Daniel was referring to the Babylonian, Persian, Greek and Roman empires—all of which dominated the world scene that included Israel.

The Apostle John's later vision rolls the four beasts into one. Daniel's beasts have a total of seven heads and ten horns, while John sees a single beast with seven heads and ten horns.

"The first was like a lion" (Dan. 7:4)	1 head	0 horns
"a second, like a bear" (Dan. 7:5)	1 head	0 horns
"another, like a leopard" (Dan. 7:6)	4 heads	0 horns
"a fourth beast, dreadful" (Dan. 7:7)	1 head	10 horns
Totals for the beasts of Daniel ch. 7	7 heads	10 horns

compare

The beast of Revelation ch. 13:1	7 heads	10 horns

While each of the four beasts Daniel saw stood for a successive empire, the composite beast John saw incorporated into one body the whole series of biblical ruling powers down through history. John's beast carried all seven heads and all ten horns on one body.

For centuries the beast of Revelation 13:1 has been identified with human governments. Respected commentator Matthew Henry indicated in his *Concise*

Commentary on the Bible, that he saw the seven-headed beast as encompassing all the Gentile world powers from the Babylonian empire through the Roman empire—those that oppressed the Jewish church or congregation prior to Christ, as well as those that persecuted Christians:

> "It appears to mean that worldly, oppressing dominion, which for many ages, even from the times of the Babylonish captivity, had been hostile to the church. The first beast then began to oppress and persecute the righteous for righteousness' sake, but they suffered most under the fourth beast of Daniel, (the Roman empire,) which has afflicted the saints with many cruel persecutions. The source of its power was the dragon. It was set up by the devil, and supported by him. . . . The world admired its power, policy and success. They paid honour and subjection to the devil and his instruments. It exercised infernal power and policy, requiring men to render that honour to creatures which belongs to God alone."

Human Government

"a beast...out of the sea, having seven heads and ten horns ...ten crowns ...like a leopard ...feet of a bear ...mouth of a lion" – Rev. 13:1-2 NKJV

"And I stood upon the sand of the sea, and saw a beast rise up out of the sea, having seven heads and ten horns, and upon his horns ten crowns, and upon his heads the name of blasphemy. And the

beast which I saw was like unto a leopard, and his feet were as the feet of a bear, and his mouth as the mouth of a lion: and the dragon gave him his power, and his seat, and great authority. And I saw one of his heads as it were wounded to death; and his deadly wound was healed: and all the world wondered after the beast. And they worshipped the dragon which gave power unto the beast: and they worshipped the beast, saying, Who is like unto the beast? who is able to make war with him?"

—Revelation 13:1-4 KJV

This composite beast, empowered by the dragon to rule the world, is a fitting picture of the governments Satan bragged about when he took Jesus up onto a mountain top and "showed unto him all the kingdoms of the world in a moment of time. And the devil said unto him, All this authority will I give thee, and the glory of them; for that is delivered unto me, and to whomsoever I will I give it. If thou, therefore, wilt worship me, all shall be thine." (Luke 4:5-7 KJV)

"a great, fiery red dragon having seven heads and ten horns, and seven diadems on his heads...that serpent of old, called the Devil and Satan" - Rev. 12:3, 9 NKJV

"all the kingdoms of the world...And the devil said...'All this authority...has been delivered to me, and I give it to whomever I wish'" - Luke 4:5-6 NKJV

Jesus rejected Satan's offer, but did not dispute the devil's role in world rulership. In fact, he regularly referred to the wicked one as "the ruler of this world" (John 12:31, 14:30, 16:11 NKJV) Satan empowered the Gentile world powers that Daniel saw as a series of beasts, including the Roman Empire that ruled the world during Jesus' earthly ministry. And Gentile powers continue to rule the world today. The composite beast John saw has been ruling the world for a long time.

Which one of its seven heads had a deadly wound that was healed? One candidate might be the Roman Empire, which could be described as dying yet coming to life again centuries later. Rome fell to the barbarians in the fifth century. But the Roman Empire rose again when Charlemagne was crowned Emperor in the year 800 A.D. The Holy Roman Empire (German: *Heiliges Römisches Reich*), with emperors crowned by the Roman pope for hundreds of years, also came to be called the Holy Roman Empire of the German Nation (*Heiliges Römisches Reich Deutscher Nation*). Its borders expanded and contracted over the centuries as conflicts were won and lost and as political alliances were forged. It was this "Reich" or Empire that Adolph Hitler referred to when dubbing his Nazi government the *Third* Reich and seeking to reclaim lost territory.

But, after speaking of this seven-headed beast with ten horns, which appears to represent human government down through the ages, John also spoke of a second beast in Revelation chapter thirteen:

"And I beheld another beast coming up out of the earth; and he had two horns like a lamb, and he spoke like a dragon. And he exerciseth all the power of the first beast before him, and causeth the earth and them who dwell on it to worship the first beast, whose deadly wound was healed. And he doeth great wonders, so that he maketh fire come down from heaven on the earth in the sight of men."

—Revelation 13:11-14 KJV

While Bible commentators over the centuries have attempted to identify this second beast, they always had to resort to metaphor to do so—interpreting the 'fire coming down from heaven' in some symbolic way, not literally. Why? Because no human government had ever been able to make fire come down from heaven to the earth in the sight of men, or as one modern translation renders it, make "fire come down from heaven to earth while people are watching." (NCV)

But some modern writers have noted that man's governments today are literally able to 'make fire come down from heaven' by waging war with airplanes, rockets and missiles. Which world power first dropped nuclear bombs from the sky? Which power is well known for calling down flaming napalm upon targets in Vietnam?

The Anglo world power, led by its two horns, Britain and America, changed the world by promoting the ideals of democracy and freedom. So, compared to other empires of the past, it looks like a lamb. It claims to promote peace and freedom, like a peaceful lamb. But the British-American conglomerate also speaks like a dragon—deceptively. These factors alone would make it a possible candidate for being the two-horned beast. (A search of the web will turn up many commentators who identify America with the beast from the earth.) But even more important is the English-speaking combo's role in the creation of "the image of the beast." Revelation goes on to say of the two-horned beast,

"And deceiveth them that dwell on the earth by the means of those miracles which he had power to do in the sight of the beast; saying to them that dwell on the earth, that they should make an image to the beast, which had the wound by a sword, and did live. And he had power to give life unto the image of the beast, that the image of the beast should both speak, and cause that as many as would not worship the image of the beast should be killed."

—Revelation 13:14-15 KJV

Some modern writers see the world body—the League of Nations and its successor organization the United Nations—as a fulfillment of the image of the beast. Since the U.N. did not come into existence until some four hundred years after the Reformation, the Reformers could hardly be expected to know about it. But did God foresee it and inspire John to write about it?

The seven-headed, ten-horned beast of Revelation 13:1, that has parts resembling a leopard, a bear and a lion, is a composite of the separate beasts Daniel described. Daniel explained that his individual beasts represented a succession of kingdoms. (Dan. 7:17, 23) So, could the "image" of the composite "beast" be some sort of miniature organizational replica of the Gentile world powers—like the United Nations?

Before the twentieth century it would have been difficult to imagine how the nations could make an "image" of the world's governments—much less cause such an image to come "life" and to "speak." But today's United Nations organization certainly is a mirror image of the kingdoms of this world, a miniature replica of the planet's political structure. The successors of the kingdoms Daniel wrote about—Babylon (Iraq), Persia (Iran), Greece and Rome (Italy)—are all represented, as well as the rest of the nations of this world. And this organizational image of the world's governments has taken on a life of its own, so that it "speaks" though official Resolutions and causes those resolutions to be enforced, ultimately through military action when necessary. Those who fail to bow to its authority may indeed be killed.

It is a matter of history that the Anglo-American power took the lead in advocating creation of the League of Nations and its successor the United Nations—a miniature image of the world's governments.

Rev. 13:1-2 portrays human government as a composite of the beasts representing successive empires in Daniel chapter 7.

The U.N., a miniature image of the world political system, actually lives and speaks.

The beasts of Daniel and the beasts of Revelation will ultimately be destroyed by the power of God. While humans may be convinced that no one can 'do battle with the beast'—they say 'you can't fight city hall'—the beastly human governments and their international organization the United Nations will all be destroyed in the coming battle of Armageddon.

What Jesus Said about Jerusalem and the End of the World

Of all the words of Jesus recorded in the Bible, about twenty-five percent of his teaching was devoted to prophecy concerning the destruction of Jerusalem, the scattering of the Jewish people worldwide, and the end of the world. He spoke of these events in advance and discussed the rewards and punishments that nations and individuals would experience.

Jesus had a number of things in mind when he spoke on these matters, and he sought to accomplish several things:

- to forewarn his first-century followers when to flee the city of Jerusalem so that they would survive its destruction by the legions of the Roman Empire

- to bring others who heard his message to repentance—both those who heard him speak in person, and those who would read his words down through the centuries

- to motivate believers to keep on the watch for Christ's return by paying attention to world events

- to let everyone know that God has already determined the outcome of human history, and that his victory over the nations is guaranteed

- to make it clear that those who obey God will be rewarded and those who ignore God will be punished when God intervenes to put an end to human rule and establish the rule of the Kingdom of God.

In Matthew's gospel, chapters 23 through 25 are devoted to these matters. But, because the discussion ranges from first century events through end times events, parts of it can be difficult to understand. The call to repentance comes through loud and clear. And the assurance of God's ultimate victory over rebellious mankind is equally clear. But the exact timing of the events foretold in these chapters is less certain—because Jesus left it that way intentionally.

The entire twenty-third chapter of Matthew's gospel is devoted to Jesus' denunciation of the Jewish religious leaders as "hypocrites" who would provoke God's punishment upon the Jewish nation within that generation. He told them,

"Verily I say unto you, All these things shall come upon this generation."

—Matthew 23:36 KJV

114

And that generation of Jews did see Jerusalem and its temple destroyed. But when Jesus again uses the expression "this generation" a few verses later at Matthew 24:34, dispensational futurists insist on applying it to a different generation at the end of the world. Many writers have tried to identify it with a particular generation in modern times. Watchtower founder Charles Taze Russell identified it with "the 'generation' from 1878 to 1914." (Russell's *Studies in the Scriptures*, vol. 4, 1908 edition, page 605) His successors in the Jehovah's Witnesses leadership changed it to "the generation that saw the events of 1914." (*Awake!* magazine, October 22, 1995, page 4). *Left Behind* authors LaHaye and Jenkins say, "we believe 'this generation' refers to those alive in 1948. It may, however, mean those alive in 1967 or those alive in some yet future war when the Jews will once again gain total control of their holy city." (Their book *Are We Living in the End Times?* page 59)

But Matthew's chapters 23 and 24 form a continuous discourse. Matthew tells us Jesus spoke the words found in chapter 23, then "went out, and departed from the temple" (24:1) and spoke the words found in chapter 24. Is it reasonable to believe that Jesus would say "this generation" to refer to his own contemporaries and then use the same term with a different meaning a few moments later?

Let's look more closely at chapter 23. What "things" are referred to here? And which "generation"? Jesus makes it unmistakably clear.

In Matthew chapter 23 Jesus was addressing the Pharisees. He called down "woes" upon them: "Woe unto you, scribes and Pharisees, hypocrites!" because they shut up the kingdom of heaven (vs. 13), because they devour widows' houses (vs. 14), because they make disciples for hell (vs. 15), because they elevate gold above the temple (vss. 16-22), because they engage in nit picking while neglecting the weightier matters of the law (vss. 23-24), and because they appear outwardly clean but are inwardly corrupt (vss. 25-33). He then reminded the Pharisees that they are "the sons of them who killed the prophets" and called them "ye generation of vipers." (vs. 31, 33) After foretelling that they would persecute and kill his disciples the same way their fathers killed the prophets, "that upon you may come all the righteous blood shed upon the earth, from the blood of righteous Abel unto the blood of Zechariah, son of Barachiah," Jesus concluded with the sentence above: "Verily I say unto you, All these things shall come upon this generation."

Clearly this was the generation that stood there in Jesus' presence, the generation he was addressing in person. The punishment for their hypocrisy and their wickedness would come upon that very generation. Just upon the scribes and Pharisees? No, in his next sentence Jesus went on to say, "Jerusalem, Jerusalem, thou that killest the prophets, and stonest them who are sent unto thee." The punishment would come upon those religious leaders and their city of Jerusalem in that very generation.

Jesus pronounced these words in or around 30 - 33 A.D., and the armies of the Roman empire brought the destruction Jesus predicted upon the city in 70 A.D., less than forty years later, within the lifetime of "this generation."

So, Jesus' use of the term "this generation" in Matthew chapter 23 defines his use of the same term in chapter 24, and makes it likely that the Great Tribulation he goes on to describe there began upon the Jewish people back in the first century, and is not an end-times event yet to come.

Likewise, Jesus' pronouncement to the Jewish religious leaders that "your house is left unto you desolate" (Matt. 23:38 KJV) is a key to understanding "the abomination of desolation" that Jesus refers to sixteen verses later.

"Verily I say unto you, all these things shall come upon this generation. O Jerusalem, Jerusalem . . . ," Jesus said. "Behold, your house is left unto you desolate." (Matt. 23:37-38 KJV) He was warning of the coming desolation of the Holy City and its temple. And he was still speaking of the same thing when he quoted Daniel about "the abomination of desolation" and the need for "them who are in Judea" to "flee into the mountains." (Matt. 24:15-16 KJV) All of this happened in 70 A.D., when the city and temple were desolated by Roman armies.

But Jesus' disciples asked him a question that complicated the issue. Their question involved not just the destruction of Jerusalem and the temple, but also the end of the world—and the timing of all these things. They asked their question shortly after Jesus finished speaking as above in the temple:

"Jesus left the temple and was walking away when his disciples came up to him to call his attention to its buildings. 'Do you see all these things?' he asked. 'I tell you the truth, not one stone here will be left on another; every one will be thrown down.' As Jesus was sitting on the Mount of Olives, the disciples came to him privately. 'Tell us,' they said, 'when will this happen, and what will be the sign of your coming and of the end of the age?' Jesus answered: 'Watch out that no one deceives you. For many will come in my name, claiming, "I am the Christ," and will deceive many. You will hear of wars and rumors of wars, but see to it that you are not alarmed. Such things must happen, but the end is still to come. Nation will rise against nation, and kingdom against kingdom. There will be famines and earthquakes in various places. All these are the beginning of birth pains.'"

—Matthew 24:1-8 NIV

So, the question the disciples asked Jesus had three parts to it:

(1) When will this happen?—the Jerusalem temple being torn down, stone by stone.

(2) What will be the sign of Jesus' coming?

(3) What will be the sign of the end of the age?

Jesus went on to answer them with a lengthy answer that covered all three parts of their question. So, it becomes necessary to discern which parts of Jesus' response refer to the first century devastation on Jerusalem, and which parts apply to his coming and the end of the world. The Gospel writers Matthew, Mark and Luke all recorded this discussion, each mentioning some different things Jesus said, but all three presenting the same basic message. The great Reformation teacher Martin Luther explained the differences among the three Gospel accounts this way, starting with a comment on Matthew, chapter 24:

> In this chapter there is a description of the end of two
> kingdoms; of the kingdom of the Jews, and also of the
> kingdom of the world. But the two Evangelists, Matthew and
> Mark, unite the two—and do not follow the order as Luke
> did, for they have nothing more in view than to relate and
> give the words of Christ, and are not concerned about what
> was said either before or after. But Luke takes special
> pains to write clearly and in the true order, and relates
> this discourse twice; first briefly in the 19th chapter,
> where he speaks of the destruction of the Jews at
> Jerusalem; afterwards in the 21st chapter he speaks of
> both, one following the other. Notice therefore that
> Matthew unites the two and at the same time conceives the
> end, both of the Jewish nation and of the world. He
> therefore cooks both into one soup. But if you want to
> understand it, you must separate and put each by itself,
> that which really treats of the Jews, and that which
> relates to the whole world.

(That quote is from Martin Luther's "Sermon for the Twenty-Fifth Sunday after Trinity; Matthew 24:15-28" from his Church Postil, first published in 1525)

The best way to grasp what Jesus said would be to read the Gospels yourself—especially Matthew chapters 23 through 25, and parallel accounts in Mark chapter 13 and Luke chapters 19 and 21. (For help comparing the three accounts side by side, you may wish to use a book like my own *Parallel Gospels in Harmony—with Study Guide*.)

One of the most controversial aspects of Jesus' prophecy is his reference to 'the abomination that causes desolation':

"So when you see standing in the holy place 'the abomination that causes desolation,' spoken of through the prophet Daniel—let the reader understand—then let those who are in Judea flee to the mountains."

—Matthew 24:15-16 NIV

Many modern teachers say that "the holy place" is a temple that will be built in Jerusalem in the future, and that a coming Antichrist will then desecrate that temple. But a closer examination of Jesus' own words places "the abomination that causes desolation" in the first century, when the Romans entered the existing temple and subsequently desolated it and the city of Jerusalem.

The immediate context should make this clear. Just a few verses before mentioning "the abomination that causes desolation," Matthew records that Jesus said, "Jerusalem, Jerusalem, . . . Look, your house is left to you desolate." (Matt. 23:38 NIV) That same "house" or temple would be left desolate by something that causes desolation—the abomination that causes desolation.

Two verses further on, at Matthew 24:1, we read that "Jesus left the temple" and the disciples called "his attention to its buildings." In the next verse, Jesus tells them about "these things" that "not one stone here will be left on another; every one will be thrown down." (vs. 2) In verse 3 the disciples ask, when will "this" happen? And thirteen verses later Jesus explains that the desolation will be accomplished by "the abomination that causes desolation." (vs. 15) Where, then, in this compact discussion, did Jesus switch from speaking about the temple he and his disciples were looking at, to bring up what would happen to a different temple in the distant future? Nowhere! The reasonable conclusion that any reader would normally reach is that the same temple forms the subject of the discussion throughout these seventeen verses. It is the same temple that is left "desolate" and faces "desolation."

The differences between Matthew's coverage and Luke's reporting on this sermon sheds light on what Jesus said and helps us understand what he meant. Writing initially for a Jewish audience familiar with the Hebrew Scriptures, Matthew included Jesus' words quoting the prophet Daniel. Luke, on the other hand, captured words that would be more understandable to his Greek-speaking audience. In Luke's parallel account we read that Jesus said,

"When you see Jerusalem surrounded by armies, you will know that its desolation is near. Then let those who are in Judea flee to the mountains."

—Luke 21:20-21 NIV

What did Jesus say would be the signal for his first-century followers and others in Judea to flee to the mountains? That signal was "armies" surrounding the city according to Luke's account, and "the abomination that causes desolation" according to Matthew's account. So, "the abomination that causes desolation" must be the Roman forces that desolated the temple and the city. Notice how they appear in the parallel accounts (KJV):

| --- | --- | --- |
| 24:15 When ye therefore shall see the abomination of desolation, spoken of by Daniel the prophet, stand in the holy place, (whoso readeth, let him understand:) 24:16 Then let them which be in Judaea flee into the mountains: 24:17 Let him which is on the housetop not come down to take any thing out of his house: 24:18 Neither let him which is in the field return back to take his clothes. | 13:14 But when ye shall see the abomination of desolation, spoken of by Daniel the prophet, standing where it ought not, (let him that readeth understand,) then let them that be in Judaea flee to the mountains: 13:15 And let him that is on the housetop not go down into the house, neither enter therein, to take any thing out of his house: 13:16 And let him that is in the field not turn back again for to take up his garment. | 21:20 And when ye shall see Jerusalem compassed with armies, then know that the desolation thereof is nigh. 21:21 Then let them which are in Judaea flee to the mountains; and let them which are in the midst of it depart out; and let not them that are in the countries enter thereinto. [17:31 "In that day, he which shall be upon the housetop, and his stuff in the house, let him not come down to take it away: and he that is in the field, let him likewise not return back.] 21:22 For these be the days of vengeance, that all things which are written may be fulfilled. |
| 24:19 And woe unto them that are with child, and to them that give suck in those days! 24:20 But pray ye that your flight be not in the winter, neither on the sabbath day: 24:21 For then shall be great tribulation, such as was not since the beginning of the world to this time, no, nor ever shall be. | 13:17 But woe to them that are with child, and to them that give suck in those days! 13:18 And pray ye that your flight be not in the winter. 13:19 For in those days shall be affliction, such as was not from the beginning of the creation which God created unto this time, neither shall be. | 21:23 But woe unto them that are with child, and to them that give suck, in those days! for there shall be great distress in the land, and wrath upon this people. 21:24 And they shall fall by the edge of the sword, and shall be led away captive into all nations: and Jerusalem shall be trodden down of the Gentiles, until the times of the Gentiles be fulfilled. |

Similarly, the "great tribulation" in Matthew is "affliction" in Mark's gospel, and Luke describes it as the Jews falling "by the edge of the sword" and being "led away captive into all nations," and Jerusalem being "trodden down of the Gentiles, until the times of the Gentiles be fulfilled." So, the "great tribulation" Jesus spoke of must refer to the centuries-long affliction of the Jewish people— from the destruction of Jerusalem until Jerusalem was taken back from Gentile control during the Six Day War of 1967.

As mentioned earlier, there is some confusion, though, because the disciples added to their question about the Temple's destruction, "and what shall be the sign of your coming, and of the end of the world?" (Matt. 24:3 KJV) Although Jesus knew, of course, that these three events—the Temple's destruction, his second coming, and the end of the world—would not be simultaneous, he went on to answer their three questions together.

Commentators offer many opinions on how the various elements of Matthew Chapter 24 should be divided and grouped together. But such forensic reconstruction is not needed, if we follow Luther's advice. We need only compare Luke's account to gain a better understanding of what Jesus meant.

The Roman forces were an abomination by virtue of the idolatrous images they carried with them, and they caused desolation by desolating Jerusalem and its temple. This understanding of Jesus' words prevailed in Protestant churches for hundreds of years, until the late 1800s and early 1900s when the writings of John Nelson Darby popularized the idea of a future seven-year tribulation, and transplanted these events from the context of the Roman destruction of the Temple to a rebuilt third temple sometime in the future.

What about Jesus' declaration that there would be strange signs in the heavens above?

"Immediately after the tribulation of those days shall the sun be darkened, and the moon shall not give her light, and the stars shall fall from heaven, and the powers of the heavens shall be shaken."

—Matthew 24:29 KJV

The stars cannot literally fall from heaven, since the stars are mammoth heavenly bodies immensely larger than the earth. The earth could literally fall onto the surface of a star, sooner than stars could actually fall to the earth. The very size relationship between earth and stars mandates that the language Jesus uses here must be figurative. Then his words fit perfectly the view that the "tribulation" here refers to the centuries-long suffering of the Jews beginning with the Roman destruction of Jerusalem, climaxing in the Holocaust, and ending with the re-establishment of the state of Israel. It was shortly after the re-establishment of Israel in 1948 that the heavens lost their power as men began to rocket into outer space. The heavenly bodies figuratively fell from the sky, as they came within mankind's reach through manned space flight. Luke reports that Jesus said,

". . . there shall be signs in the sun, and in the moon, and in the stars . . . for the powers of heaven shall be shaken."

—Luke 21:25-26 KJV

While the Jews were returning to the Promised Land after their centuries-long tribulation, the scientists who had worked on Adolph Hitler's V-1 and V-2 rockets began working for the victorious allied powers. Soon test pilots flew experimental jets above earth's atmosphere for the first time in human history. Soviet Russia put its Sputnik satellite into orbit in 1957, followed shortly by the first manned space flights.

The Jews re-took Jerusalem from Gentile hands in 1967, and immediately after that in 1969 a series of six Apollo space flights began bringing men to the moon. Humans circled the moon, taking pictures of its hidden far side, and landed there to plant an American flag on this heavenly body. It was as if the heavens had lost their power; they were no longer unreachable, but had now fallen beneath human feet. There were signs in the sun, moon and stars that had never before been seen.

Jesus went on to say,

"But as the days of Noah were, so shall the coming of the Son of man be. For as in the days that were before the flood they were eating and drinking, marrying and giving in marriage, until the day that Noah entered into the ark, and knew not until the flood came, and took them all away, so shall also the coming of the Son of man be. Then shall two be in the field; the one shall be taken, and the other left. . . . Watch, therefore; for ye know not what hour your Lord doth come."

—Matthew 24:37-42 KJV

Ever since Jesus gave this admonition, Christians have been watching for his coming. He said it would be like the days of Noah. God's favored people were saved in the Ark, and the disobedient were destroyed by the flood—at the same time. The Lord said his coming would be like that. Will you be one of those who survive?

"Therefore be ye also ready: for in such an hour as ye think not the Son of man cometh."

— Matthew 24:44 KJV

Have you read Jesus' words in their entirety, in the Bible itself? Reading my discussion above—or reading what other modern writers have to say about Jesus' message—can never be as beneficial as reading what Jesus himself actually said. You will be blessed if you put this book down for a while and pick up the Bible to read it prayerfully. Ask God for insight and understanding so that you can obey Jesus' teaching. He will answer such a prayer, and will give you the help you need. Jesus' sermons and parables will help you understand what is coming, and will help you prepare to survive.

How to Survive

When the first humans rebelled against God, it would appear that God had two options for populating this planet as he had originally intended: either destroy the rebels and start over again, or redeem some of their offspring.

How easy it would have been to annihilate Adam and Eve and then create a new man from the dust of the ground and a new woman from his rib! But God chose the more difficult alternative of tolerating human rebellion for thousands of years, during which time he would lay the necessary groundwork through his Chosen People, send his only begotten Son as the savior and redeemer of fallen mankind, and nurture a church of the Messiah's followers. Finally, he would collect the harvest from all this effort—people from every nation—and cleanse the earth from wickedness and corruption in a fiery battle of Armageddon. In the end there would remain a redeemed human race living godly lives in peace and harmony in God's kingdom.

That battle of Armageddon is near, and survival is guaranteed only to those who follow the instructions outlined in the Bible.

The Hebrew writers of the Old Testament presented elements of the divine plan, shedding light on it progressively down through the ages. They pointed forward to the coming of the Anointed One or Messiah, laid the basis for identifying him, and hinted at what he would accomplish. Called "Christ" from the Greek word for "Anointed One," Jesus showed how all of those prophecies fit together and how they would result in human salvation—not just survival to live a few more years, but eternal life with no more death.

The way to everlasting life that Jesus proclaimed was not through church or organizational membership or through accurate knowledge of the Scriptures— although both of these enter into it. In order to gain life, people had to come to Jesus personally. Under the "new covenant" he instituted, there would be no other way to the Father, except through Jesus. "I am the way, the truth, and the life. No one comes to the Father except through Me." (John 14:6 New King James Version)

This can be understood best by looking first at the "old covenant" that God had established centuries earlier with Israel. Jews were in a special relationship with God, through this formal agreement or covenant, by virtue of being members of the nation of Israel. This arrangement was to be superseded by a new covenant at some future time, according to the prophecy of Jeremiah, chapter 31.

"'The time is coming,' declares the LORD, 'when I will make a new covenant with the house of Israel and with the house of Judah. It will not be like the covenant I made with their forefathers when I took them by the hand to lead them out of Egypt, because they broke my covenant, though I was a husband to them,' declares the LORD."

—Jeremiah 31:31-32 NIV

Under this new covenant "'they will all know me, from the least of them to the greatest,' declares the LORD. 'For I will forgive their wickedness and will remember their sins no more.'" (verse 34 NIV) All sorts of sinful people— even prostitutes and corrupt tax collectors—came to Jesus and received forgiveness of their sins. The forgiveness was a free gift, not earned by good works. This angered the Jewish religious leaders who wanted people to seek righteousness through the works program they had outlined to them. But those who accepted Jesus as their Savior rejoiced and were overjoyed to feel the burden of sin lifted off their shoulders.

Besides promising forgiveness of sins, the prophecy of Jeremiah 31:34 also went on to say, "'they will all know me, from the least of them to the greatest,' declares the LORD." This did not mean just additional details of knowledge or information about God, but actually knowing God personally. How? By personally living with Jesus Christ, the Son of God, on a day-to-day basis. When Philip asked to see the Father, "Jesus answered: 'Don't you know me, Philip, even after I have been among you such a long time? Anyone who has seen me has seen the Father. How can you say, "Show us the Father"?.'" (John 14:9 NIV)

"The Son is the radiance of God's glory and the exact representation of his being," according to Hebrews 1:3 (NIV). So, those who actually lived with Jesus could get to know God in this new intimate way that was not possible for people who just "study the Scriptures" as the Pharisees did. (John 5:39 NIV) The 'knowing the LORD' that Jeremiah prophesied about is this sort of close, personal relationship with God through His Son.

And Jeremiah was not offering a new covenant for just a handful of people in the First Century. Rather, it would be God's way of dealing with people from that time onward. For example, Paul's relationship with God through His Son began when Jesus appeared to Paul on the road to Damascus. Later on, Paul told of occasions when "Lord stood at my side and gave me strength" (2 Tim. 4:17 NIV), and when Paul spoke to the Lord about his "thorn in my flesh." (2 Cor. 12:7-9) As a zealous Jew, Paul had had a relationship with God before, but only from a distance. Now, as a Christian, he really knew God.

The different ways in which the two covenants were instituted set the pattern. The old covenant was established with Moses conveying messages back and forth between God and the people, while the people stood at a distance from Mount Sinai where God appeared:

"When the people saw the thunder and lightning and heard the trumpet and saw the mountain in smoke, they trembled with fear. They stayed at a distance and said to Moses, 'Speak to us yourself and we will listen. But do not have God speak to us or we will die.' Moses said to the people, 'Do not be afraid. God has come to test you, so that the fear of God will be with you to keep you from sinning.' The people remained at a distance, while Moses approached the thick darkness where God was."

—Exodus 20:18-21 NIV

By contrast, the new covenant was established at the Last Supper with the Son of God sitting privately to share a meal with his twelve apostles. The setting was so intimate that John leaned back onto Jesus' breast to ask him a question. (John 13:25) That intimacy was to continue, as Jesus made clear in the words that he prayed in the hearing of his apostles:

"'My prayer is not for them alone. I pray also for those who will believe in me through their message, that all of them may be one, Father, just as you are in me and I am in you. May they also be in us . . . Righteous Father, though the world does not know you, I know you, and they know that you have sent me. I have made you known to them, and will continue to make you known in order that the love you have for me may be in them and that I myself may be in them.'"

—John 20:20-26 NIV

Stephen saw Jesus in a vision during his trial. A short while later, after his trial broke up and he was brought outside the city, Stephen called out to Jesus.

"And as they were stoning Stephen, he prayed, 'Lord Jesus, receive my spirit.' And he knelt down and cried with a loud voice, 'Lord, do not hold this sin against them.'"

—Acts 7:59-60 RSV

There is no indication that the earlier vision was repeated then. Rather, Stephen had an on-going relationship with Jesus and felt free to call upon him.

Were Paul and Stephen unique in having a personal relationship with the Son of God, calling upon Jesus in time of need? Evidently not, since Paul described Christians as "all those everywhere who call on the name of our Lord Jesus Christ." (1 Cor 1:2 NIV)

Jesus promised his continuing presence with his disciples:

"'For where two or three are gathered together in my name, there am I in the midst of them.'"

—Matthew 18:20 KJV

In fact, we have Jesus' promise that

"'He that hath my commandments, and keepeth them, he it is that loveth me: and he that loveth me shall be loved of my Father, and I will love him, and will manifest myself to him. . . . and my Father will love him, and we will come unto him, and make our abode with him.'"

—John 14:21-23 KJV

The Living Bible paraphrases it this way:

"'When I come back to life again . . . I will only reveal myself to those who love and obey me. The Father will love them too, and we will come to them and live with them.'"

—vss. 20-23

Jesus does not usually reveal himself to people today in a blinding light, as he appeared to Paul on the road to Damascus. Rather, it is more as described here:

"God has sent the Spirit of his Son into our hearts, crying, 'Abba! Father!'"

—Galatians 4:6 RSV

At first I was afraid to approach God in prayer to confess my sin and ask Jesus into my heart as my Savior and Lord. Due to my earlier religious training, I was skeptical of such a 'sinner's prayer' and was even afraid of receiving a demonic spirit instead. But then I read Jesus' words at Luke 11:10-13:

"'For every one who asks receives, and he who seeks finds, and to him who knocks it will be opened. What father among you, if his son asks for a fish, will instead of a fish give him a serpent; or if he asks for an egg, will give him a scorpion? If you then, who are evil, know how to give good gifts to your children, how much more will the heavenly Father give the Holy Spirit to those who ask him!'"

—Luke 11:10-13 RSV

So, I prayed and received Jesus' spirit into my heart. I experienced a personal fulfillment of Galatians 4:6 and came to know God as my Father in a way that I had never known before.

So, the Gospel of the Christian Scriptures, the new covenant that Jeremiah 31 foretold, is not a new set of doctrines to learn or new facts about God (although some erroneous doctrines may need to be un-learned). Rather, it is a salvation that includes a new life right now, as a new creature by virtue of being born again and living a new Spirit-filled life.

Jesus introduced this new life when He told Nicodemus,

"'Verily, verily, I say unto thee, Except a man be born again, he cannot see the Kingdom of God. . . . Except a man be born of water and of the Spirit, he cannot enter into the kingdom of God. That which is born of the flesh is flesh; and that which is born of the Spirit is spirit. Marvel not that I said unto thee, Ye must be born again.'"

—John 3:3-7 KJV

All of those who come into the new covenant undergo this change:

"You, however, are controlled not by your sinful nature but by the Spirit, if the Spirit of God lives in you. And if anyone does not have the Spirit of Christ, he does not belong to Christ. But if Christ is in you, your body is dead because of sin, yet your spirit is alive because of righteousness. And if the Spirit of him who raised Jesus from the dead is living in you, he who raised Christ from the dead will also give life to your mortal bodies through his Spirit, who lives in you. . . . Those who are led by the Spirit of God are sons of God. For you did not receive a spirit that makes you a slave again to fear, but you received the Spirit who makes you sons. And by him we cry, 'Abba, Father.' The Spirit himself testifies with our spirit that we are God's children."

—Romans 8:9-11, 14-16 NIV

When you are born again, you are a babe in Christ at first. And just as toddlers tend to fall while learning to walk, so it is with learning to walk in the Spirit. But the Father will help you grow as his child. You will form a longing for his written Word, the Bible, and the Holy Spirit will teach you as you read. You will see more and more clearly that Jesus could not be merely the first angelic creation, as some cults teach, but that He is, as doubting Thomas finally came to believe, "My Lord and my God!" (John 20:28 KJV)

Besides learning more about God and growing in love for Him, you will also come to see yourself as part of the body of Christ. This is "the church of the firstborn, whose names are written in heaven." (Heb. 12:23 NIV) The true church, Christ's body, crosses denominational lines and includes individuals both in and out of the various religious organizations that men have set up. It is composed of all those who look to Christ as Head, who have been "baptized by one Spirit into one body." (1 Cor. 12:13 NIV)

"Now the body is not made up of one part but of many. If the foot should say, 'Because I am not a hand, I do not belong to the body,' it would not for that reason cease to be part of the body. . . . The eye cannot say to the hand, 'I don't need you!'" (1 Cor. 12:12-21 NIV) So, we need our brothers and sisters in Christ, even if we see ourselves as quite different from them.

It may be difficult at first to adopt this scriptural view of our brothers in Christ:

"If a person's faith is not strong enough, welcome him all the same without starting an argument. People range from those who believe they may eat any sort of meat to those whose faith is so weak they dare not eat anything except vegetables. Meat eaters must not despise the scrupulous. On the other hand, the scrupulous must not condemn those who feel free to eat anything they choose, since God has welcomed them. It is not for you to condemn someone else's servant. . . . If one man keeps certain days as holier than others, and another considers all days to be equally holy, each must be left free to hold his own opinion."

—Romans 14:1-5 JB

If you accept this view of the brotherhood, then you will find it easier to fellowship with Christians from other backgrounds.

Ask the Lord to guide you into the fellowship he wants you to be in. He will answer your prayer. Of course, he may put you into a local congregation like the one in Corinth, where the gifts of the Spirit were being misused and where the Lord's Supper was not being celebrated properly. (1 Cor. 14:23, 11:20) Or, he may send you into a church like the one in Pergamum, where corrupt practices and false teachings prevailed among some members. (Rev. 2:14, 15) Or, you may find yourself in a congregation like the one in Sardis that had "a reputation of being alive" but was actually "dead." (Rev. 3:1 NIV) Such experiences can help you to grow and to deepen your personal relationship with Jesus as Lord. "Bear what you have to bear as 'chastening'—as God's dealing with you as sons," part of your training from the Father. (Heb. 12:7 J.B. Phillips)

We all should admit, as Paul the Apostle did, that

"We can see and understand only a little about God now, as if we were peering at his reflection in a poor mirror; but someday we are going to see him in his completeness, face to face. Now all that I know is hazy and blurred, but then I will see everything clearly, just as clearly as God sees into my heart right now."

—1 Corinthians 13:12 LB

So, while 'accurate knowledge' of every detail is not yet available, it is the Christian's privilege to "know" God through a close, personal relationship with

Jesus Christ. If you have not yet done so, tell God right now that you need Jesus as your Savior, and receive him as your Lord. He invites you:

"'Come to me, all of you who are tired from carrying heavy loads, and I will give you rest.'"

—Matthew 11:28 TEV

"'I will never turn away anyone who comes to me.'"

—John 6:37 TEV

"My sheep listen to my voice; I know them, and they follow me. I give them eternal life, and they shall never perish; no one will snatch them out of my hand."

—John 10:27-28 NIV

"'I am the resurrection and the life. He who believes in me will live, even though he dies.'"

—John 11:25 NIV

.

Many "Christians" Won't Survive

A prominent Christian leader spends many years preaching the Gospel message and denouncing corruption, sin and sexual immorality. Then it comes to light that he has been leading a double life, practicing the very things he has denounced in his sermons. How do people react? How does God react? Many church members immediately jump to such a man's defense, arguing that God forgives everything. 'He is saved,' they say, 'covered by the blood of Christ,' so he is in no danger. But they say such things because they believe what popular religious books teach rather than what Jesus taught.

Jesus himself said that "many" who claim to be Christians and who preach in Jesus' name and who even accomplish great things in Jesus' name—but who live a lifestyle the Bible condemns—will be surprised to hear Jesus reject them and turn them away from the kingdom of God:

"'Not every one who says to me, "Lord, Lord," shall enter the kingdom of heaven, but he who does the will of my Father who is in heaven. On that day many will say to me, "Lord, Lord, did we not prophesy in your name, and cast out demons in your name, and do many mighty works in your name?" And then will I declare to them, "I never knew you; depart from me, you evildoers."'"

—Matthew 7:21-23 RSV

The Apostle Paul made it clear to the members of churches he preached to that they would be misleading themselves if they thought they could continue to practice things God condemns, and still enter the kingdom of God. He wrote,

". . . don't you know that the unrighteous will not inherit the Kingdom of God? Don't be deceived. Neither the sexually immoral, nor idolaters, nor adulterers, nor male prostitutes, nor homosexuals, nor thieves, nor covetous, nor drunkards, nor slanderers, nor extortioners, will inherit the Kingdom of God.

"Such were some of you, but you were washed. But you were sanctified. But you were justified in the name of the Lord Jesus, and in the Spirit of our God."   —1 Corinthians 6:9-11

When they turned to Jesus for salvation, those people were cleansed of the sins that would have kept them out of God's kingdom. But, if they persisted in those sins, they would have been disqualified. Even though they called on his name, Jesus would tell them, "I never knew you; depart from me, you evildoers." (Matt. 7:23 RSV)

The world around us today has changed, but God has not changed. So, even though their church may say it is okay for people to live like that, Jesus does not say it's okay. He says he will reject them.

But many churches have given up preaching the real Jesus, the Jesus of the Bible. Instead, they preach a fictitious Jesus—a Jesus of popular culture who loves everyone and everything, forgives everyone and everything and doesn't require anything of anyone. It is just as the Apostle Paul warned:

"...the time will come when people will not listen to the true teaching but will find many more teachers who please them by saying the things they want to hear." —2 Timothy 4:3 NCV

People want to hear about this easy-going Jesus of popular culture, not the real Jesus who told a man he healed, "Stop sinning or something worse may happen to you." (John 5:14 NIV)

Paul warned that already in his day some churches accepted false teachers preaching another Jesus, a Jesus different from the real Jesus:

"You are very patient with anyone who comes to you and preaches a different Jesus from the one we preached. You are very willing to accept a spirit or gospel that is different from the Spirit and Good News you received from us." —2 Corinthians 11:4

This same thing has been happening for centuries, with the result that there are many millions of people today who think they are following Jesus, or who say they are following him, but who are not following the real Jesus at all. Whole churches are misled by pastors and teachers who say it is okay to do the things Jesus said not to do.

And even in churches that recognize what the Bible says about sin, it has become popular to excuse churchgoers or relatives who practice sin. 'I know they aren't living right,' it is said, 'but they love the Lord.'

Do such practicers of sin really love the Lord? No, not according to what the Lord himself said. Jesus said it repeatedly, to emphasize the point:

"'If you love me, keep my commands. . . .

"'Whoever has my commands and keeps them is the one who loves me. . . .

"'Anyone who loves me will obey my teaching. . . .

"'Anyone who does not love me will not obey my teaching.'"

—John 14:15-24 NIV

So those who live sinful lives contrary to Jesus' teachings do not love the Lord—regardless of the words or emotions they may express. Jesus said such people do not love him. If they don't obey him, they don't love the Lord.

But the popular view today ignores what Jesus actually taught, and instead asserts that people who live sinful lives are in no danger of punishment if "they love the Lord." And the Jesus of popular culture loves and accepts everything and everyone, not requiring obedience. People who follow this make-believe Jesus may feel happy, but they won't be happy for long. Their problem is that the real Jesus is alive. He rose from the grave and is active today among his people. And he is coming again. He is the same risen Christ who sent this message to the Christian church in the city of Thyatira:

"'I know what you do. I know about your love, your faith, your service, and your patience. I know that you are doing more now than you did at first.

"'But I have this against you: You let that woman Jezebel spread false teachings. . . . by her teaching she leads my people to take part in sexual sins . . . I have given her time to change her heart and turn away from her sin, but she does not want to change. So I will throw her on a bed of suffering. . . . I will also kill her followers. Then all the churches will know that I am the One who searches hearts and minds, and I will repay each one of you for what you have done.'" —Revelation 2:19-23 NCV

There are Jezebels like that in many of today's churches. Those who follow them will someday have to face the real Jesus, and it will not be a pleasant encounter.

What Happens Next?

The Bible provides a considerable amount of detail concerning the dramatic events that will occur at the time of the end. However, the details are scattered among many different prophetic passages throughout numerous books of the Old and New Testaments.

Zechariah's prediction that Jerusalem would become a problem for the whole world, and that the nations would unite to impose their solution, is found in the opening verses of his twelfth chapter. Zechariah continues to discuss events related to Jerusalem through the end of chapter fourteen. However, it is not clear whether all of these developments are chronological, or even closely related in time. Here are some highlights:

"'On that day I will make the leaders of Judah like a firepot in a woodpile, like a flaming torch among sheaves. They will consume right and left all the surrounding peoples, but Jerusalem will remain intact in her place.'"

—Zechariah 12:6 NIV

Could this be a reference to the time since 1948, when the small Jewish state has been victorious in one war after another, fought against Arab neighbors who were determined to eliminate the state of Israel?

"'On that day the LORD will shield those who live in Jerusalem, so that the feeblest among them will be like David, and the house of David will be like God, like the Angel of the LORD going before them. On that day I will set out to destroy all the nations that attack Jerusalem.'"

—Zechariah 12:8-9 NIV

Chapter fourteen seems to imply that the final attack on Jerusalem by all the nations will be successful at first, before God steps in to reverse their apparent victory:

"'I will gather all the nations to Jerusalem to fight against it; the city will be captured, the houses ransacked, and the women raped. Half of the city will go into exile, but the rest of the people will not be taken from the city. Then the LORD will go out and fight against those nations, as he fights in the day of battle.'"

—Zechariah 14:2-3 NIV

But we know for sure that victory belongs to God, and that he will eventually triumph over the nations.

"This is the plague with which the LORD will strike all the nations that fought against Jerusalem: Their flesh will rot while they are still standing on their feet, their eyes will rot in their sockets, and their tongues will rot in their mouths. On that day men will be stricken by the LORD with great panic. Each man will seize the hand of another, and they will attack each other."

—Zechariah 14:12-14 NIV

The apostle John was imprisoned on a Roman penal island called Patmos, when he received his divine revelation of future events. He told of the time when the leaders of all the nations would assemble their forces at the place in Israel called Armageddon, or Mount Megiddo:

". . . they go out to the kings of the whole world, to gather them for the battle on the great day of God Almighty. . . . Then they gathered the kings together to the place that in Hebrew is called Armageddon."

—Revelation 16:14-16 NIV

John's Revelation goes on to describe the victory of the Kingdom of God over the kingdoms of men:

"I saw heaven standing open and there before me was a white horse, whose rider is called Faithful and True. With justice he judges and makes war. His eyes are like blazing fire, and on his head are many crowns. He has a name written on him that no one knows but he himself. He is dressed in a robe dipped in blood, and his name is the Word of God.

"The armies of heaven were following him, riding on white horses and dressed in fine linen, white and clean. Out of his mouth comes a sharp sword with which to strike down the nations. 'He will rule them with an iron scepter.' He treads the winepress of the fury of the wrath of God Almighty. On his robe and on his thigh he has this name written: KING OF KINGS AND LORD OF LORDS.

"And I saw an angel standing in the sun, who cried in a loud voice to all the birds flying in midair, 'Come, gather together for the great supper of God, so that you may eat the flesh of kings, generals, and mighty men, of horses and their riders, and the flesh of all people, free and slave, small and great.' Then I saw the beast and the kings of the earth and their armies gathered together to make war against the rider on the horse and his army. But the beast was

captured, and with him the false prophet . . . The rest of them were killed with the sword that came out of the mouth of the rider on the horse, and all the birds gorged themselves on their flesh."

These prophecies must be pieced together with those found scattered elsewhere in the Old and New Testaments. The Hebrew prophet Joel recorded these warnings from God about the armies of all the nations converging on the valley of Jehoshaphat in Israel:

"I will also gather all nations, and will bring them down into the valley of Jehoshaphat, and will plead with them there for my people and for my heritage Israel, whom they have scattered among the nations, and parted my land. And they have cast lots for my people; and have given a boy for an harlot, and sold a girl for wine, that they might drink. Yea, and what have ye to do with me, O Tyre, and Zidon, and all the coasts of Palestine? will ye render me a recompence? and if ye recompense me, swiftly and speedily will I return your recompence upon your own head."

—Joel 3:2-4 KJV

Joel's inspired description of God Almighty's intervention on behalf of Jerusalem truly inspires fear and awe—with the action again focusing on Jerusalem and on the valley of Jehoshaphat in Israel:

"Proclaim ye this among the Gentiles; Prepare war, wake up the mighty men, let all the men of war draw near; let them come up: Beat your plowshares into swords, and your pruninghooks into spears: let the weak say, I am strong. Assemble yourselves, and come, all ye heathen, and gather yourselves together round about:

"thither cause thy mighty ones to come down, O LORD. Let the heathen be wakened, and come up to the valley of Jehoshaphat: for there will I sit to judge all the heathen round about. Put ye in the sickle, for the harvest is ripe: come, get you down; for the press is full, the fats overflow; for their wickedness is great.

"Multitudes, multitudes in the valley of decision: for the day of the LORD is near in the valley of decision.

"The sun and the moon shall be darkened, and the stars shall withdraw their shining. The LORD also shall roar out of Zion, and utter his voice from Jerusalem; and the heavens and the earth shall shake: but the LORD will be the hope of his people, and the strength of the children of Israel. So shall ye know that I am the LORD your God dwelling in Zion, my holy mountain: then shall

Jerusalem be holy, and there shall no strangers pass through her any more. . . . But Judah shall dwell for ever, and Jerusalem from generation to generation."

—Joel 3:9-17, 20 KJV

The prophet Isaiah likewise uses powerful language to describe the coming battle when God will "gather all nations" and wage war from heaven against humans who make themselves his enemies:

"Rejoice with Jerusalem and be glad for her . . . For this is what the LORD says: 'I will extend peace to her like a river, and the wealth of nations like a flooding stream; . . . and you will be comforted over Jerusalem.' . . . the hand of the LORD will be made known to his servants, but his fury will be shown to his foes. See, the LORD is coming with fire, and his chariots are like a whirlwind; he will bring down his anger with fury, and his rebuke with flames of fire. For with fire and with his sword the LORD will execute judgment upon all men, and many will be those slain by the LORD. . . . 'And I, because of their actions and their imaginations, am about to come and gather all nations and tongues, and they will come and see my glory . . . ,' says the LORD. 'And they will go out and look upon the dead bodies of those who rebelled against me; their worm will not die, nor will their fire be quenched, and they will be loathsome to all mankind.'"

—Isaiah 66:10-24 NIV

Similar powerful language is used by New Testament writers. Peter, for example, reminds readers of the earlier prophecies and of the global deluge of Noah's day as proof that God can and will intervene again in the affairs of mankind:

"I want you to recall the words spoken in the past by the holy prophets and the command given by our Lord and Savior through your apostles. First of all, you must understand that in the last days scoffers will come, scoffing and following their own evil desires. They will say, 'Where is this "coming" he promised? Ever since our fathers died, everything goes on as it has since the beginning of creation.' But they deliberately forget that long ago by God's word the heavens existed and the earth was formed out of water and by water. By these waters also the world of that time was deluged and destroyed. By the same word the present heavens and earth are reserved for fire, being kept for the day of judgment and destruction of ungodly men."

—2 Peter 3:2-7 NIV

These prophecies are not provided so that we will know ahead of time exactly what will happen and exactly when. Rather, they are provided so that we will know that God knows exactly what will happen, and so that this knowledge will motivate us to put our trust in him. Moses explained that some information belongs to God alone, and that the information God gives us is sufficient for us to do what is right:

"The secret things belong to the LORD our God, but the things revealed belong to us and to our children forever, that we may follow all the words of this law." —Deuteronomy 29:29 NIV

Prophecy is usually best understood in retrospect. We may have twenty-twenty hindsight in our understanding of fulfilled prophecy, but seldom do we have twenty-twenty foresight as to how the remaining prophecies will be fulfilled.

This fact is abundantly clear from the failure on the part of the Jewish religious leaders to recognize clearly all the prophecies about the Messiah and to understand them correctly before he appeared. Jesus called his followers' attention to many of those prophecies and how they applied to him and were fulfilled by him. And the apostles' writings went on to explain how many more versus in the Old Testament applied to the Messiah, and pointed out how those were fulfilled by Jesus. Yet, serious Jewish students of Scripture had been unable to discern the correct scenario: that the Messiah would not arrive as a conquering hero, but would appear humble and would be killed and would only later return in power.

The same may well be true with the prophecies about the final conflict over Jerusalem. We may best understand them after the events take place.

The Apostle Paul wrote,

"Now, brothers and sisters, about times and dates we do not need to write to you, for you know very well that the day of the Lord will come like a thief in the night. While people are saying, 'Peace and safety,' destruction will come on them suddenly, as labor pains on a pregnant woman, and they will not escape.

"But you, brothers and sisters, are not in darkness so that this day should surprise you like a thief. You are all children of the light and children of the day. We do not belong to the night or to the darkness. So then, let us not be like others, who are asleep, but let us be awake and sober."

—1 Thessalonians 5:1-6 NIV

Jesus devoted a significant portion of his teaching to the subject of his return and the end of the world. Many of his parables are devoted to this theme, describing how people would be caught by surprise, and would be rewarded or punished at that time. You may wish to read, for example, the parable of the ten virgins, the parable of the talents, and the parable of the sheep and the goats—all found in the twenty-fifth chapter of the Gospel of Matthew—and the parable of the faithful and wise servant at the end of the twenty-fourth chapter.

Jesus encouraged us to

"'Therefore keep watch, because you do not know on what day your Lord will come.

. . . be ready, because the Son of Man will come at an hour when you do not expect him.'"   —Matthew 24:42-44 NIV

We can "be ready" by living the way the Bible teaches us to live, and we can "keep watch" by eagerly praying for Christ's return and by paying attention to world events that point to the imminence of his coming. Which events? When Jesus told them about the coming destruction of the temple in Jerusalem, his disciples asked him, "Tell us, when will these things be? What is the sign of your coming, and of the end of the age?" (Matt. 24:3) Jesus answered them with a lengthy discussion of future world events, recorded for us in Matthew chapters 24-25, Mark chapter 13 and Luke chapter 21.

After speaking about armies surrounding and destroying Jerusalem, and the Jewish people being scattered worldwide, Jesus went on to speak of future events that would lead up to his return in power:

"'There will be signs in the sun, moon, and stars; and on the earth anxiety of nations, in perplexity for the roaring of the sea and the waves; men fainting for fear, and for expectation of the things which are coming on the world: for the powers of the heavens will be shaken. Then they will see the Son of Man coming in a cloud with power and great glory. But when these things begin to happen, look up, and lift up your heads, because your redemption is near.'"   —Luke 21:23-28

Meanwhile we can take comfort in these words of Jesus:

"When these things begin to happen, stand up and raise your heads, because your salvation is near."

—Luke 21:28 TEV

So, we can confidently expect a final conflict between God and the nations—a conflict that will somehow involve Israel and Jerusalem—but we must content ourselves with knowing what the final outcome will be, without knowing all the details of what will happen between now and then.

America's Role

American president Woodrow Wilson is credited with inventing and promoting the formation of the League of Nations, which immediately gave Britain an international Mandate to rule Palestine after the First World War. And the United States of America played a decisive role in defeating the Nazi government of Adolph Hitler in the Second World War, before it could finish its methodical extermination of the Jewish people in death camps created for that specific purpose. The U.S. likewise played a key role in forming the United Nations organization at the end of that war, and in the U.N. plan to partition Palestine into a Jewish state and an Arab state.

Did the Bible prophesy that the United States would do all these things during the final days of this world? No, at least not explicitly. Of course, we might learn in retrospect, after all the apocalyptic the events of the book of Revelation unfold, that some of the cryptic language there contained hidden allusions to America. But, there are certainly no clear references naming the U.S.A. in Bible prophecy. Nevertheless, we may see prophetic shadows of an American role in the two-horned beast of Revelation chapter 13 that looks like a lamb and speaks like a dragon, and in the two wings of the eagle given to the woman of Revelation chapter 12, to save her (Israel) from destruction.

Moreover, there is plenty of biblical precedent for a Gentile super-power that would play the role America has been playing until now.

Bible history relates the major role that the Egyptian world power played in the origin of ancient Israel. Joseph, the eleventh son of the man Jacob whom God renamed Israel, served for years as prime minister of Egypt. As a gesture of favor toward his prime minister, Pharaoh king of Egypt invited Joseph's father Israel and Joseph's brothers, the heads of the future twelve tribes, to reside in Egyptian territory with their families and their flocks and herds. It was there during their hundreds of years of alien residence in Egypt, that the Jewish people grew in population to the size of a small nation. Then a later king of Egypt began to fear this growing nationality, and so enslaved them and became their oppressor. The book of Exodus in the Bible relates the story of their liberation from Egypt by means of the mighty hand of God.

Will America similarly switch sides as Egypt did? Will America cease being Israel's ally, and become its enemy instead? Bible prophecy suggests that this will happen.

The ancient neo-Babylonian empire, like modern-day Iraq under its dictator Saddam Hussein, was Israel's enemy. But, after conquering Israel and Judah, and deporting the Jewish population, the king of Babylon installed some bright young Jewish men in positions of power in his government. In fact, the Hebrew prophet Daniel was given the position of prime minister in the Babylonian government. Daniel's Jewish friends Shadrach, Meshach and Abednego were made governors over certain Babylonian territories. And it was due to his high position that Daniel was able to deliver God's message personally to the king of Babylon—the message that led to our modern day expression "the handwriting on the wall"—when Babylon was about to fall to its arch enemy, the Medo-Persian empire.

Certain Jews later rose to high positions in that empire of Media and Persia that succeeded Babylon as the super-power dominating the Middle East. But there were also enemies in high places. The Bible book of Esther relates the story of the powerful Persian prime minister Haman who tried to exterminate the Jewish people more than two thousand years before Hitler's attempt. The Jews were rescued by means of King Ahasuerus's Jewish wife, Queen Esther, whose uncle Mordecai became prime minister to replace Haman.

During the twentieth year of the reign of Persian emperor Artaxerxes, another Jewish man, Nehemiah, had the job of royal cup-bearer. One day, when handing the monarch his glass of wine to drink, Nehemiah looked sad, and the king sympathetically asked him why. The servant replied that he was sad over the condition of Jerusalem, and the king granted Nehemiah's request to return to Jerusalem with imperial authority to rebuild the city and its temple.

Considering this long history of world powers that served as political allies of the Jewish state, or that came to the aid of Israel at one time or another, it should not surprise us that the British empire would be instrumental in the return of the Jews to the Promised Land in fulfillment of Bible prophecy. This took the form of the Balfour declaration issued toward the end of the First World War, committing the British government to the establishment of a Jewish state. Nor should it be surprising that the British and American world powers would combine to defeat Adolph Hitler's attempt to exterminate the Jewish people immediately prior to their return to the Promised Land.

In fact, viewed from a biblical perspective, the First World War was about that Balfour declaration and the transfer of the Promised Land from Muslim to British control. And the Second World War was about preserving the Jews from annihilation. If God were to use a modern-day prophet to write additional books to be added to the Bible cannon, that is certainly how the account would read in reference to the two world wars.

During recent years America has been Israel's one and only powerful ally, but that will soon change. The Bible foretells that, when Jerusalem becomes a problem for the whole world, all of the nations will share in attacking Israel. So, America must, no doubt, be included in those nations arrayed against Israel at that time.

It should not be difficult to conceive of this happening. As noted earlier in this book, different presidential administrations in Washington have taken different positions vis-a-vis Israel over the years. Some have attempted to play the role of mediator by maintaining official neutrality between the Jews and their Arab neighbors. Others have presented themselves as staunch allies of the Jewish state. A small swing in public opinion is all that it would take to allow an American president to side with the rest of the United Nations against Israel.

On June 8, 1967, during the Arab-Israeli Six Day War, a lightly-armed American warship that was engaged in intelligence gathering in international waters off the Sinai Peninsula was attacked by Israeli ships and aircraft, resulting in the deaths of thirty-four American military personnel and the wounding of a hundred seventy-one others. Israel claimed it was an accident—that the U.S.S. Liberty was mistaken for an Egyptian vessel—and U.S. President Lyndon Johnson accepted that explanation. The Israeli government quickly paid reparations to the injured and to the families of the sailors who had been killed. Since then, a number of writers have alleged that the attack was actually deliberate, launched because Israel was concerned that the intelligence gathered by the spy ship might be shared with some of its Arab enemies in that life-or-death struggle. (See www.USSLiberty.org for articles and links on this topic.)

Could a similar incident sway American opinion against Israel in a future confrontation? Or perhaps an Israeli pre-emptive strike against Iran or some other enemy will wreak such destruction that American popular opinion will turn against Israel. Or perhaps Israel will be the first to use nuclear weapons in a Middle East war, provoking an American reaction quite different from when their own atomic bombs wiped out the Japanese cities of Hiroshima and Nagasaki in 1945.

In any case, the reversal of America's role towards Israel does not depend on our speculation. Prophecy makes it plain that all of the nations of the world will turn against Israel and will unite for the final attack on Jerusalem.

Scripture does not state that the nations attacking Israel in this final act of rebellion against God will come in the form of United Nations forces wearing blue helmets. The prophet Zechariah indicates merely that Jerusalem will become a problem for the whole world, and that the nations will be united in their attack. "Jerusalem will be a heavy stone burdening the world," and "all the nations of the earth unite in an attempt" to impose their solution. (Zechariah 12:3 LB) A formal "United Nations organization" is not actually cited by name in the Bible, just as the "United States of America" is not named.

Even if the attack does prove to be sponsored by the U.N. organization through Security Council and/or General Assembly resolutions, it may not consist of forces wearing the blue helmets common to international peacekeeping operations. It could be a military force mobilized by a coalition of willing states, acting on a mandate from the Security Council, such as the one the United States had hoped to assemble to remove Saddam Hussein from power in Iraq, or similar to the U.S.-led United Nations force used in the Korean conflict of the 1950's.

In any case, it will be a force of "united nations" in the generic sense, whether or not it turns out to be an official military action under the auspices of the United Nations organization as we know it today.

The purpose of this book is not to speculate on the exact nature of such an attack, nor how it will be organized politically. Rather, my aim in writing is to call attention to the fact that Jerusalem has become a problem for the whole world, as Zechariah foretold, and that political moves are afoot among the nations and specifically within the framework of the United Nations organization, to impose the will of the world in a final solution for the status of Jerusalem.

Although some may see that as a terrifying prospect, the Bible offers reason for hope. The Hebrew prophets speak of a time of world peace to follow this international attack on Jerusalem. The New Testament speaks of the Jewish Messiah Jesus Christ ruling in peace "for a thousand years" following his victory in that battle. (Rev. 20:4) Jesus' words recorded in Matthew chapter 24, Mark chapter 13 and Luke chapter 21 tell us the signs to look for, and Jesus concluded, "When these things begin to take place, stand up and lift up your heads, because your redemption is drawing near . . . when you see these things happening, you know that the kingdom of God is near." (Luke 21:28-31 NIV)

Nations United and Resolved

Zechariah's prophecy that "all the nations of the earth will be gathered against" Jerusalem (Zech. 12:3 NASB) parallels similar predictions recorded by Joel and the apostle John, which speak all the nations sending their armies to the region. "For, behold, in those days, and in that time, when I shall bring back the captivity of Judah and Jerusalem, I will gather all nations, and will bring them down into the valley of Jehoshaphat; and I will enter into judgment with them there," says the Lord, according to Joel 3:1-2. (The Holy Scriptures, The Jewish Publication Society of America) A demonic summons goes out to "all the kings of the world to call them together for the war of the Great Day of God the Almighty. . . . They called the kings together at the place called, in Hebrew, Armageddon." (Revelation 16:14, 16 The Jerusalem Bible; footnote: "Megiddo mountains")

But Bible prophecy is not the only reason to expect a united international military force to converge on Jerusalem. There is also a modern political paper trail indicating that the nations of the world have already begun laying a legal foundation to justify such a move. First, the nations began to unite in the form of the League of Nations and, later, the United Nations organization. Then these organizations began passing resolutions regarding Palestine, Israel and Jerusalem. And, more recently, the nations began granting the United Nations more and more power to act militarily.

The League of Nations made Britain's Palestine Mandate one of its first official acts—granting Britain international authority to administer the land—and its successor organization, the United Nations, passed Resolution 181 in 1947 calling for the division of Palestine into Jewish and Arab states, but also demanding international control over Jerusalem. Since then, there have been more U.N. resolutions on Israel and Palestine than on any other region of the world. These have consistently called for the Jews to vacate all or part of Jerusalem, for Israel not to claim the city as its capital, or for Jerusalem to be internationalized under a governor appointed by the United Nations.

The nations have thus spent decades "uniting" for the prophesied attack and drawing up resolutions to legalize it; now all that remains is the enforcement.

General Assembly resolutions express world opinion but do not carry the threat of enforcement through blue-helmet-wearing U.N. peacekeeping forces. Security Council resolutions can be enforced militarily, but a lone veto cast by the United States has effectively blocked most Security Council measures hostile to Israel. If that veto were to be removed, the path would be open for the nations to have their way in regard to Jerusalem.

The complete text of all U.N. resolutions can be viewed at the United Nations official website at www.UN.org. The General Assembly and Security Council resolutions on Israel and Palestine can by found at the U.N. web site by surfing to the URL http://domino.UN.org/UNISPAL.NSF/ and clicking on links for "Documents by Type" and then "Resolution." The sheer size of the list of documents found there is truly impressive.

Without going into the details of all these resolutions here, it may suffice to quote the full text of one in particular. Toward the end of the year 2002 the U.N. General Assembly passed Resolution 57/111 on Jerusalem, which states that "the international community, through the United Nations, has a legitimate interest in the question of the City of Jerusalem" and that "any actions taken by Israel to impose its laws, jurisdiction and administration on the Holy City of Jerusalem are illegal and therefore null and void and have no validity whatsoever." Here is the text of that resolution, as copied from the U.N. web site:

57/111. Jerusalem

The General Assembly,

Recalling its resolution 181 (II) of 29 November 1947, in particular its provisions regarding the City of Jerusalem,

Recalling also its resolution 36/120 E of 10 December 1981 and all subsequent resolutions, including resolution 56/31 of 3 December 2001, in which it, inter alia, determined that all legislative and administrative measures and actions taken by Israel, the occupying Power, which have altered or purported to alter the character and status of the Holy City of Jerusalem, in particular the so-called "Basic Law" on Jerusalem and the proclamation of Jerusalem as the capital of Israel, were null and void and must be rescinded forthwith,

Recalling further Security Council resolutions relevant to Jerusalem, including resolution 478 (1980) of 20 August 1980, in which the Council, inter alia, decided not to recognize the "Basic Law" and called upon those States which had established diplomatic missions in Jerusalem to withdraw such missions from the Holy City,

Expressing its grave concern at any action taken by any body, governmental or non-governmental, in violation of the above-mentioned resolutions,

Reaffirming that the international community, through the United Nations, has a legitimate interest in the question of the City of Jerusalem and the protection of the unique spiritual and religious dimension of the city, as foreseen in relevant United Nations resolutions on this matter,

Having considered the report of the Secretary-General,12

1. Reiterates its determination that any actions taken by Israel to impose its laws, jurisdiction and administration on the Holy City of Jerusalem are illegal and therefore null and void and have no validity whatsoever;

2. Deplores the transfer by some States of their diplomatic missions to Jerusalem in violation of Security Council resolution 478 (1980), and calls once more upon those States to abide by the provisions of the relevant United Nations resolutions, in conformity with the Charter of the United Nations;

3. Stresses that a comprehensive, just and lasting solution to the question of the City of Jerusalem should take into account the legitimate concerns of both the Palestinian and Israeli sides and should include internationally guaranteed provisions to ensure the freedom of religion and of conscience of its inhabitants, as well as permanent, free and unhindered access to the holy places by the people of all religions and nationalities;

4. Requests the Secretary-General to report to the General Assembly at its fifty-eighth session on the implementation of the present resolution.

66th plenary meeting

3 December 2002

RECORDED VOTE ON RESOLUTION 57/111: 154-5-6

In favour : Afghanistan, Algeria, Andorra, Antigua and Barbuda, Argentina, Armenia, Australia, Austria, Azerbaijan, Bahamas, Bahrain, Bangladesh, Barbados, Belarus, Belgium, Belize, Bhutan, Bolivia, Bosnia and Herzegovina, Botswana, Brazil, Brunei Darussalam, Bulgaria, Burkina Faso, Burundi, Cambodia, Canada, Cape Verde, Chile, China, Colombia, Comoros, Congo, Côte d'Ivoire, Croatia, Cuba, Cyprus, Czech Republic, Democratic People's Republic of Korea, Democratic Republic of the Congo, Denmark, Djibouti, Dominican Republic, Ecuador, Egypt, Eritrea, Estonia, Ethiopia, Fiji, Finland, France, Gabon, Gambia, Georgia, Germany, Ghana, Greece, Grenada, Guinea, Guyana, Haiti, Honduras, Hungary, Iceland, India, Indonesia, Iran (Islamic Republic of), Ireland, Italy, Jamaica, Japan, Jordan, Kazakhstan, Kenya, Kuwait, Kyrgyzstan, Lao People's Democratic Republic, Latvia, Lebanon, Lesotho, Libyan Arab Jamahiriya, Liechtenstein, Lithuania, Luxembourg, Malaysia, Maldives, Mali, Malta, Mauritania, Mauritius, Mexico, Monaco, Morocco, Mozambique, Myanmar, Namibia, Nepal, Netherlands, New Zealand, Nicaragua, Nigeria, Norway, Oman, Pakistan, Panama, Paraguay, Peru, Philippines, Poland, Portugal, Qatar, Republic of Korea, Republic of Moldova, Romania, Russian Federation, Saint Lucia, Saint Vincent and the

Grenadines, San Marino, Sao Tome and Principe, Saudi Arabia, Senegal, Seychelles, Sierra Leone, Singapore, Slovakia, Slovenia, Somalia, South Africa, Spain, Sri Lanka, Sudan, Suriname, Sweden, Switzerland, Syrian Arab Republic, Tajikistan, Thailand, the former Yugoslav Republic of Macedonia, Togo, Trinidad and Tobago, Tunisia, Turkey, Uganda, Ukraine, United Arab Emirates, United Kingdom of Great Britain and Northern Ireland, United Republic of Tanzania, Uruguay, Venezuela, Viet Nam, Yemen, Yugoslavia, Zambia, Zimbabwe

Against : Costa Rica, Israel, Marshall Islands, Micronesia (Federated States of), United States of America

Abstaining : Albania, Nauru, Papua New Guinea, Solomon Islands, Tuvalu , Vanuatu

Besides passing resolutions, the United Nations organization has also been heavily involved in the peace process, especially in connection with the so-called "roadmap" for peace, sponsored jointly by the "Quartet" of the United States, the United Nations, Russia and the European Union.

The previous phase of the peace process broke down when discussions reached the stage of determining the status of Jerusalem. That resulted in renewed conflict between Israel and the Palestinians. Now with the rest of the world and the United Nations organization involved this time through the "roadmap," if the peace process breaks down again over Jerusalem, this could have consequences that are more far reaching. If progress continues to the point of an actual peace on the ground with some sort of international peacekeeper presence to enforce that peace in and around Jerusalem, a breakdown and renewal of hostilities at that point could involve the United Nations militarily.

Here is the text of that "roadmap for peace," as posted on the official U.N. website at http://www.UN.org/media/main/roadmap122002.html Note how the final phase of the roadmap calls for international involvement in determining the ultimate status of Jerusalem.

a Performance-Based Roadmap

to a Permanent Two-State Solution to the Israeli-Palestinian Conflict

The following is a performance-based and goal-driven roadmap, with clear phases, timelines, target dates, and benchmarks aiming at progress through reciprocal steps by the two parties in the political, security, economic, humanitarian, and institution-building fields, under the auspices of the Quartet. The destination is a final and comprehensive settlement of the Israel-Palestinian conflict by 2005, as presented in President Bush's speech of 24 June, and welcomed by the EU, Russia and the UN in the 16 July and 17 September Quartet Ministerial statements.

A two state solution to the Israeli-Palestinian conflict will only be achieved through an end to violence and terrorism, when the Palestinian people have a leadership acting decisively against terror and willing and able to build a practicing democracy based on tolerance and liberty, and through Israel's readiness to do what is necessary for a democratic Palestinian state to be established, and a clear, unambiguous acceptance by both parties of the goal of a negotiated settlement as described below. The Quartet will assist and facilitate implementation of the plan, starting in Phase I, including direct discussions between the parties as required. The plan establishes a realistic timeline for implementation. However, as a performance-based plan, progress will require and depend upon the good faith efforts of the parties, and their compliance with each of the obligations outlined below. Should the parties perform their obligations rapidly, progress within and through the phases may come sooner than indicated in the plan. Non-compliance with obligations will impede progress.

A settlement, negotiated between the parties, will result in the emergence of an independent, democratic, and viable Palestinian state living side by side in peace and security with Israel and its other neighbors. The settlement will resolve the Israel-Palestinian conflict, and end the occupation that began in 1967, based on the foundations of the Madrid Conference, the principle of land for peace, UNSCRs 242, 338 and 1397, agreements previously reached by the parties, and the initiative of Saudi Crown Prince Abdullah - endorsed by the Beirut Arab League Summit - calling for acceptance of Israel as a neighbor living in peace and security, in the context of a comprehensive settlement. This initiative is a vital element of international efforts to promote a comprehensive peace on all tracks, including the Syrian-Israeli and Lebanese-Israeli tracks.

The Quartet will meet regularly at senior levels to evaluate the parties' performance on implementation of the plan. In each phase, the parties are expected to perform their obligations in parallel, unless otherwise indicated.

Phase I:

Ending Terror And Violence, Normalizing Palestinian Life,

and Building Palestinian Institutions

Present to May 2003

In Phase I, the Palestinians immediately undertake an unconditional cessation of violence according to the steps outlined below; such action should be accompanied by supportive measures undertaken by Israel. Palestinians and Israelis resume security cooperation based on the Tenet work plan to end violence, terrorism, and incitement through restructured and effective Palestinian security services. Palestinians undertake comprehensive political reform in preparation for statehood, including drafting a Palestinian constitution, and free, fair and open elections upon the basis of those measures. Israel takes all necessary steps to help normalize Palestinian life. Israel withdraws from Palestinian areas occupied from September 28, 2000 and the two sides restore the status quo that existed at that time, as security performance and cooperation progress. Israel also freezes all settlement activity, consistent with the Mitchell report.

At the outset of Phase I:

Palestinian leadership issues unequivocal statement reiterating Israel's right to exist in peace and security and calling for an immediate and unconditional ceasefire to end armed activity and all acts of violence against Israelis anywhere. All official Palestinian institutions end incitement against Israel.

Israeli leadership issues unequivocal statement affirming its commitment to the two-state vision of an independent, viable, sovereign Palestinian state living in peace and security alongside Israel, as expressed by President Bush, and calling for an immediate end to violence against Palestinians everywhere. All official Israeli institutions end incitement against Palestinians.

Security

· Palestinians declare an unequivocal end to violence and terrorism and undertake visible efforts on the ground to arrest, disrupt, and restrain individuals and groups conducting and planning violent attacks on Israelis anywhere.

· Rebuilt and refocused Palestinian Authority security apparatus begins sustained, targeted, and effective operations aimed at confronting all those engaged in terror and dismantlement of terrorist capabilities and infrastructure. This includes commencing confiscation of illegal weapons and consolidation of security authority, free of association with terror and corruption.

· GOI takes no actions undermining trust, including deportations, attacks on civilians; confiscation and/or demolition of Palestinian homes and property, as a punitive measure or to facilitate Israeli construction; destruction of Palestinian institutions and infrastructure; and other measures specified in the Tenet work plan.

· Relying on existing mechanisms and on-the-ground resources, Quartet representatives begin informal monitoring and consult with the parties on establishment of a formal monitoring mechanism and its implementation.

· Implementation, as previously agreed, of U.S. rebuilding, training and resumed security cooperation plan in collaboration with outside oversight board (U.S.-Egypt-Jordan). Quartet support for efforts to achieve a lasting, comprehensive cease-fire.

Ø All Palestinian security organizations are consolidated into three services reporting to an empowered Interior Minister.

Ø Restructured/retrained Palestinian security forces and IDF counterparts progressively resume security cooperation and other undertakings in implementation of the Tenet work plan, including regular senior-level meetings, with the participation of U.S. security officials.

· Arab states cut off public and private funding and all other forms of support for groups supporting and engaging in violence and terror.

· All donors providing budgetary support for the Palestinians channel these funds through the Palestinian Ministry of Finance's Single Treasury Account.

· As comprehensive security performance moves forward, IDF withdraws progressively from areas occupied since September 28, 2000 and the two sides restore the status quo that existed prior to September 28, 2000. Palestinian security forces redeploy to areas vacated by IDF.

Palestinian Institution-Building

· Immediate action on credible process to produce draft constitution for Palestinian statehood. As rapidly as possible, constitutional committee circulates draft Palestinian constitution, based on strong parliamentary democracy and cabinet with empowered prime minister, for public comment/debate. Constitutional committee proposes draft document for submission after elections for approval by appropriate Palestinian institutions.

· Appointment of interim prime minister or cabinet with empowered executive authority/decision-making body.

· GOI fully facilitates travel of Palestinian officials for PLC and Cabinet sessions, internationally supervised security retraining, electoral and other reform activity, and other supportive measures related to the reform efforts.

· Continued appointment of Palestinian ministers empowered to undertake fundamental reform. Completion of further steps to achieve genuine separation of powers, including any necessary Palestinian legal reforms for this purpose.

· Establishment of independent Palestinian election commission. PLC reviews and revises election law.

· Palestinian performance on judicial, administrative, and economic benchmarks, as established by the International Task Force on Palestinian Reform.

· As early as possible, and based upon the above measures and in the context of open debate and transparent candidate selection/electoral campaign based on a free, multi-party process, Palestinians hold free, open, and fair elections.

· GOI facilitates Task Force election assistance, registration of voters, movement of candidates and voting officials. Support for NGOs involved in the election process.

· GOI reopens Palestinian Chamber of Commerce and other closed Palestinian institutions in East Jerusalem based on a commitment that these institutions operate strictly in accordance with prior agreements between the parties.

Humanitarian Response

· Israel takes measures to improve the humanitarian situation. Israel and Palestinians implement in full all recommendations of the Bertini report to improve humanitarian conditions, lifting curfews and easing restrictions on movement of persons and goods, and allowing full, safe, and unfettered access of international and humanitarian personnel.

· AHLC reviews the humanitarian situation and prospects for economic development in the West Bank and Gaza and launches a major donor assistance effort, including to the reform effort.

· GOI and PA continue revenue clearance process and transfer of funds, including arrears, in accordance with agreed, transparent monitoring mechanism.

Civil Society

· Continued donor support, including increased funding through PVOs/NGOs, for people to people programs, private sector development and civil society initiatives.

Settlements

· GOI immediately dismantles settlement outposts erected since March 2001.

· Consistent with the Mitchell Report, GOI freezes all settlement activity (including natural growth of settlements).

Phase II: Transition

June 2003-December 2003

In the second phase, efforts are focused on the option of creating an independent Palestinian state with provisional borders and attributes of sovereignty, based on the new constitution, as a way station to a permanent status settlement. As has been noted, this goal can be achieved when the Palestinian people have a leadership acting decisively against terror, willing and able to build a practicing democracy based on tolerance and liberty. With such a leadership, reformed civil institutions and security structures, the Palestinians will have the active support of the Quartet and the broader international community in establishing an independent, viable, state.

Progress into Phase II will be based upon the consensus judgment of the Quartet of whether conditions are appropriate to proceed, taking into account performance of both parties. Furthering and sustaining efforts to normalize Palestinian lives and build Palestinian institutions, Phase II starts after Palestinian elections and ends with possible creation of an independent Palestinian state with provisional borders in 2003. Its primary goals are continued comprehensive security performance and effective security cooperation, continued normalization of Palestinian life and institution-building, further building on and sustaining of the goals outlined in Phase I, ratification of a democratic Palestinian constitution, formal establishment of office of prime minister, consolidation of political reform, and the creation of a Palestinian state with provisional borders.

• International Conference: Convened by the Quartet, in consultation with the parties, immediately after the successful conclusion of Palestinian elections, to support Palestinian economic recovery and launch a process, leading to establishment of an independent Palestinian state with provisional borders.

Ø Such a meeting would be inclusive, based on the goal of a comprehensive Middle East peace (including between Israel and Syria, and Israel and Lebanon), and based on the principles described in the preamble to this document.

Ø Arab states restore pre-intifada links to Israel (trade offices, etc.).

Ø Revival of multilateral engagement on issues including regional water resources, environment, economic development, refugees, and arms control issues.

• New constitution for democratic, independent Palestinian state is finalized and approved by appropriate Palestinian institutions. Further elections, if required, should follow approval of the new constitution.

• Empowered reform cabinet with office of prime minister formally established, consistent with draft constitution.

· Continued comprehensive security performance, including effective security cooperation on the bases laid out in Phase I.

· Creation of an independent Palestinian state with provisional borders through a process of Israeli-Palestinian engagement, launched by the international conference. As part of this process, implementation of prior agreements, to enhance maximum territorial contiguity, including further action on settlements in conjunction with establishment of a Palestinian state with provisional borders.

· Enhanced international role in monitoring transition, with the active, sustained, and operational support of the Quartet.

· Quartet members promote international recognition of Palestinian state, including possible UN membership.

Phase III:

Permanent Status Agreement

and End of the Israeli-Palestinian Conflict

2004 - 2005

Progress into Phase III, based on consensus judgment of Quartet, and taking into account actions of both parties and Quartet monitoring. Phase III objectives are consolidation of reform and stabilization of Palestinian institutions, sustained, effective Palestinian security performance, and Israeli-Palestinian negotiations aimed at a permanent status agreement in 2005.

· Second International Conference: Convened by Quartet, in consultation with the parties, at beginning of 2004 to endorse agreement reached on an independent Palestinian state with provisional borders and formally to launch a process with the active, sustained, and operational support of the Quartet, leading to a final, permanent status resolution in 2005, including on borders, Jerusalem, refugees, settlements; and, to support progress toward a comprehensive Middle East settlement between Israel and Lebanon and Israel and Syria, to be achieved as soon as possible.

· Continued comprehensive, effective progress on the reform agenda laid out by the Task Force in preparation for final status agreement.

· Continued sustained and effective security performance, and sustained, effective security cooperation on the bases laid out in Phase I.

· International efforts to facilitate reform and stabilize Palestinian institutions and the Palestinian economy, in preparation for final status agreement.

• Parties reach final and comprehensive permanent status agreement that ends the Israel-Palestinian conflict in 2005, through a settlement negotiated between the parties based on UNSCR 242, 338, and 1397, that ends the occupation that began in 1967, and includes an agreed, just, fair, and realistic solution to the refugee issue, and a negotiated resolution on the status of Jerusalem that takes into account the political and religious concerns of both sides, and protects the religious interests of Jews, Christians, and Muslims worldwide, and fulfills the vision of two states, Israel and sovereign, independent, democratic and viable Palestine, living side-by-side in peace and security.

• Arab state acceptance of full normal relations with Israel and security for all the states of the region in the context of a comprehensive Arab-Israeli peace.

Note that the status of Jerusalem is to be addressed during the final phase of the roadmap, under the guidance of an "International Conference." The roadmap calls for "a negotiated resolution on the status of Jerusalem that takes into account the political and religious concerns of both sides, and protects the religious interests of Jews, Christians, and Muslims worldwide."

As of this writing the roadmap has already faced many obstacles, with violence continuing while Israel and the Palestinian Authority both hold back from fulfilling obligations spelled out in the agreement. The agreed-upon dates have passed, and goals have been postponed. To what extent there will be further breakdowns along the road, delaying the full implementation of the roadmap to peace, remains to be seen. It also remains to be seen whether this latest peace process involving the United Nations will end up fulfilling the biblical prophecies discussed in this book.

The maneuvering leading up to Armageddon could be brief, or it could last several years. But it is clear from the U.N. documents presented earlier in this book and above in this chapter that the nations of the world are already united and resolved in their determination to impose their will on Jerusalem—just as the Bible predicted.

Why Do Churches Fail to Preach about the End?

Jesus devoted a significant portion of his preaching and teaching to the subject of his second coming—his return in power, and the end of the world. Similarly, his apostles and disciples who wrote the New Testament under divine inspiration also spoke at length about Christ's return. But the subject is seldom mentioned in churches today. Why?

After his death and resurrection, Jesus appeared alive to his followers over the course of some weeks. Then, as they watched, he rose into the sky until he disappeared from their sight. Two angels told the disciples,

"'You men of Galilee, why do you stand looking into the sky? This Jesus, who was received up from you into the sky will come back in the same way as you saw him going into the sky.'" —Acts 1:11

How often do we hear this mentioned in church?

Jesus himself spoke repeatedly to the disciples about his return, his second coming. It will not be like his humble birth in a barn or his submissive death on the cross. Rather, Jesus said he will return with great power and glory,

"'Then they will see the Son of Man coming in clouds with great power and glory. Then he will send out his angels, and will gather together his chosen ones from the four winds, from the ends of the earth to the ends of the sky.'" —Mark 13:26-27

How many pastors quote this passage in their Sunday sermons?

Jesus will return as King of the kingdom of God. When he was put on trial before the high court of the Jews, and the high priest demanded to know whether Jesus was the Christ, the Son of God,

"Jesus said to him, 'You have said it. Nevertheless, I tell you, after this you will see the Son of Man sitting at the right hand of Power, and coming on the clouds of the sky.'" —Matthew 26:64

Jesus knew that the Jewish religious leaders would understand this to be a reference to the book of Daniel, where the prophet wrote,

"I saw in the night visions, and behold, there came with the clouds of the sky one like a son of man, and he came even to the ancient of days, and they brought him near before him. There was given

him dominion, and glory, and a kingdom, that all the peoples, nations, and languages should serve him: his dominion is an everlasting dominion, which shall not pass away, and his kingdom that which shall not be destroyed." —Daniel 7:13-14

This was a major thrust of Jesus' preaching and teaching, but it is seldom if ever mentioned in Christian churches. Why?

Many of Jesus' parables are devoted to the subject of his return in power, describing how people would be caught by surprise, and would be rewarded or punished at that time. You may wish to read, for example, the parable of the ten virgins, the parable of the talents, and the parable of the sheep and the goats—all found in the twenty-fifth chapter of the Gospel of Matthew—and the parable of the faithful and wise servant at the end of the twenty-fourth chapter. You may wish to read them on your own, because they are seldom read in church. Or, if they are read, they are used as a springboard to discuss some other topic, not the topic of Christ's return and the end of the world.

Jesus encouraged us to

"'Therefore keep watch, because you do not know on what day your Lord will come. . . . be ready, because the Son of Man will come at an hour when you do not expect him.'" —Matthew 24:42-44 NIV

This was a powerful exhortation that Jesus repeated to his audiences. But how often is it repeated in Christian churches today?

We can "be ready" by living our lives the way the Bible teaches us to live, and we can "keep watch" by eagerly praying for Christ's return and by paying attention to world events that point to the imminence of his coming. Which events? The events discussed in this book. Looking into the prophecies and their fulfillment is part of our keeping watch and being ready.

But watching for Christ's return is not popular—not even among church-goers. Why not?

After Jesus' death and resurrection his apostles and other early followers faithfully preached the message he had taught them, and they recorded this message in their writings that now make up the Bible's New Testament. But, even at that time there were portions of the Christian message that were unpopular and that people did not want to hear. For example, when the Apostle Paul shared the Gospel message with Roman governor Felix, the governor listened gladly to the part about putting faith in Christ, but he did not want to hear the part about the lifestyle Jesus commanded his followers to live, and about God's coming judgment:

"He listened to Paul talk about believing in Christ Jesus. But Felix became afraid when Paul spoke about living right, self-control, and

the time when God will judge the world. He said, 'Go away now.
When I have more time, I will call for you.'"   —Acts 24:24-25 NCV

Powerful and influential people today often behave in much the same way as governor Felix, responding favorably to appealing parts of the Gospel message, but not wanting to hear the parts about living right, self-control, and the time when God will judge the world. In so-called "Christian" countries, such people may even join a church and consider themselves to be Christian. As major financial contributors, or as people who do a lot of the work in the church, they may tell the pastor they don't want to hear him preach on certain topics that they find offensive, or that they think might offend others in the audience. The Apostle Paul faithfully preached the full force of Jesus' message, even though he was jailed and eventually killed for doing so, but many church leaders over the centuries have compromised the message to please their listeners. "For the time will come when men will not put up with sound doctrine. Instead, to suit their own desires, they will gather around them a great number of teachers to say what their itching ears want to hear." (2 Tim. 4:3 NIV)

Likewise today, the pastor of a church may feel obliged to leave out offensive topics from his Sunday messages, in order to keep his job and to avoid losing church members. (I have heard even Bible-believing pastors of Bible-believing churches admit that they have done this—leaving out mention of money, or of certain sins, or leaving out the full force of God's judgment message—at the request of influential members of their church, or out of fear of losing their job.)

Some churches today that call themselves Christian preach a Jesus who loves and accepts everyone and everything, who doesn't require anything of anyone— and who isn't ever really coming again to call people to account.

But that isn't the real Jesus, the Jesus of the Bible.

The real Jesus would be ridiculed and opposed if he showed up to preach on earth today. The main theme of his preaching was a call to 'Repent!' That word is found most commonly today in cartoons comically portraying a foolish-looking crazy person in a beard and white robe carrying a placard with that message. The call to repent is seen as a joke. And if preached seriously from the pulpit, then people are offended, because they don't want to be told that their lifestyle is condemned by God.

Matthew says this about how Jesus began his ministry:

"Jesus began to preach, and to say, 'Repent!'"   —Matthew 4:17

And Luke shows that Jesus concluded his ministry on earth with the same theme:

"that repentance and remission of sins should be preached in his name to all the nations."   —Luke 24:47

Decades later when the Gospel message had already spread throughout the Mediterranean area, resulting in the formation of many Christian churches, the risen Christ appeared to the then aged Apostle John in a lengthy vision that John wrote down in the Bible book now called the Apocalypse or Revelation. It is a book of prophecy detailing, in symbolic language, events leading up to the end of this world.

In that vision Jesus commanded John to send messages to seven major Christian churches of that day, the churches in "Ephesus, Smyrna, Pergamum, Thyatira, Sardis, Philadelphia and Laodicea." (Rev. 1:11) The messages to most of those churches included a call for their members to "Repent!"—even though they were already Christians:

To the church in the city of Ephesus, Jesus said:

". . . Repent and do the things you did at first. If you do not repent, I will come to you and remove your . . ."   —Revelation 2:5 NIV

To the church in the city of Pergamum, he said:

". . . Repent therefore! Otherwise, I will soon come to you and will fight . . ."   —Revelation 2:16 NIV

To the church in the city of Sardis, the risen Christ said:

". . . Remember, therefore, what you have received and heard; obey it, and repent. But if you do not wake up, I will come like a thief, and you will not know at what time I will come to you. . . ."

—Revelation 3:3 NIV

To the church in city of Laodicea, Jesus said:

". . . Those whom I love I rebuke and discipline. So, be earnest, and repent. . . ."   —Revelation 3:19 NIV

Jesus calls five of the seven churches to "repent" for straying, in various ways, from following him. (I purposely quoted just a few words from the messages to these churches—enough to show that Jesus was calling their members to repent—but you would benefit from reading these messages in their completeness in Revelation chapters 2 and 3.)

So, Jesus calls on us to "Repent!"—change our hearts and lives—when we first turn to him to as our Savior and Lord. And he repeatedly calls Christians to "Repent!" even later during our walk with him as his followers. When we regularly read the Bible and prayerfully think about the things it says and how those words apply to our lives, God's Holy Spirit shows us the changes we need to make to grow up as God's adopted children and to become more like Jesus.

The remainder of the book of Revelation presents a long series of visions full of signs and symbols: "A great and wondrous sign appeared in heaven" (12:1 NIV), "Then another sign appeared in heaven" (12:3 NIV), "And I saw another sign in heaven" (15:1 KJV) The exact meanings of these signs and symbols have been the subject of debate for centuries, but the basic overall message is clear: God will intervene in human affairs to put an end to man's governments and to establish the worldwide rule of the Kingdom of God. In the process, God sends one plague or disaster after another—diseases, scorching heat, pollution of the seas and rivers, destruction of "a third of the trees" (Rev. 8:7 NCV), and so on—to punish rebellious mankind and call people to repent. "The other people who were not killed by these terrible disasters still did not change their hearts . . . and turn away from murder or evil magic, from their sexual sins or stealing." (Rev. 9:20-21 NCV) Or, as another translation words it, "The rest of mankind who were not killed by these plagues still did not . . . repent of their murders, their magic arts, their sexual immorality or their thefts." (NIV)

The Revelation goes on to show the world's governments and armies suffering defeat at a "place that is called Armageddon in the Hebrew language" (Rev. 16:16 NCV), after which Christ rules for a thousand years.

The message that people need to repent, and that God is going to judge the world, has never been popular. But it has been the message of the prophets and the Apostles down through the ages. It may not be popular in churches today, but it was the message Christ gave to his followers to preach. And it is the message that people in today's world need to hear, as the foretold events are beginning to occur.

Are You Ready?

So, does all of this mean that you should quit your job, stop mowing your front lawn, and spend your time parading downtown carrying a poster that proclaims, "The End Is Near!"?

No, but it may call for some less severe adjustments on your part.

Is there some unfinished business between you and God? Have you been putting it off until after you have finished raising the children? Or, have you been delaying until after your new business endeavor has gotten up and running and becomes firmly established? Or, have you been waiting until your busy career winds down and retirement gives you more time to spend in the Scriptures and in prayer?

If so, then the things discussed in this book should make you reconsider your priorities. There may not be time to leave God until later. Instead of leaving God waiting in the wings, you may need to re-order your life's interests so as to move your relationship with God to center stage.

Are you still unconvinced that God exists as the Creator of the universe and the divine Author of the human genetic code? But, does the neo-Darwinian theory of evolution leave you unsatisfied because it fails to explain how complex structures with interdependent parts could spring into existence by accident? And are you left wondering how living creatures come complete with genetic blueprints if there was no intelligent designer to write those complete instructions for designing and building them? Have you been leaving a complete investigation of the issues involved until some future time? Hopefully this book will motivate you to take the time now. There are many resources that will help you in your quest for an answer. But, don't leave the question hanging.

People will react differently to the urgency of the times. Some will value the answers to these questions, and some won't. Some will be diligent in their investigation, and some will not. Some will allow the Bible's message to change their lives, and some will not. Jesus put it this way in the parable of the sower or planter of seed:

"'Behold, a sower went forth to sow; And when he sowed, some [seeds] fell by the way side, and the fowls came and devoured them up: Some fell upon stony places, where they had not much earth: and forthwith they sprung up, because they had no deepness of earth: And when the sun was up, they were scorched; and because

they had no root, they withered away. And some fell among thorns; and the thorns sprung up, and choked them: But other fell into good ground, and brought forth fruit, some an hundredfold, some sixtyfold, some thirtyfold. Who hath ears to hear, let him hear.'"

—Matthew 13:3-9 KJV

What did Jesus mean by this parable? He explains it himself, and the explanation makes clear that it applies to people and how they respond to his message:

"'Hear ye therefore the parable of the sower. When any one heareth the word of the kingdom, and understandeth it not, then cometh the wicked one, and catcheth away that which was sown in his heart. This is he which received seed by the way side. But he that received the seed into stony places, the same is he that heareth the word, and anon with joy receiveth it; Yet hath he not root in himself, but dureth for a while: for when tribulation or persecution ariseth because of the word, by and by he is offended. He also that received seed among the thorns is he that heareth the word; and the care of this world, and the deceitfulness of riches, choke the word, and he becometh unfruitful. But he that received seed into the good ground is he that heareth the word, and understandeth it; which also beareth fruit, and bringeth forth, some an hundredfold, some sixty, some thirty.'"

—Matthew 13:18-23 KJV

Some will treasure their relationship with God and will do whatever it takes to gain or repair that relationship. Jesus further explained it this way:

"'Again, the kingdom of heaven is like unto treasure hid in a field; the which when a man hath found, he hideth, and for joy thereof goeth and selleth all that he hath, and buyeth that field. Again, the kingdom of heaven is like unto a merchant man, seeking goodly pearls: Who, when he had found one pearl of great price, went and sold all that he had, and bought it.'"

—Matthew 13:44-46 KJV

Is your appreciation on a level with that of the man who found the treasure or the merchant who found the pearl? It is a matter of the heart—your appreciation for what God has done for you. You don't have to become a theologian, in order to please God. He is not looking for intellectuals. Jesus exclaimed,

"'I thank thee, O Father, Lord of heaven and earth, because thou hast hid these things from the wise and prudent, and hast revealed them unto babes."

—Matthew 11:25

Similarly, the Apostle Paul wrote:

"Christ did not send me to baptize, but to preach the gospel—not with words of human wisdom, lest the cross of Christ be emptied of its power. For the message of the cross is foolishness to those who are perishing, but to us who are being saved it is the power of God.

"For it is written: 'I will destroy the wisdom of the wise; the intelligence of the intelligent I will frustrate.' Where is the wise man? Where is the scholar? Where is the philosopher of this age? Has not God made foolish the wisdom of the world?

"For since in the wisdom of God the world through its wisdom did not know him, God was pleased through the foolishness of what was preached to save those who believe. Jews demand miraculous signs and Greeks look for wisdom, but we preach Christ crucified: a stumbling block to Jews and foolishness to Gentiles, but to those whom God has called, both Jews and Greeks, Christ the power of God and the wisdom of God.

"For the foolishness of God is wiser than man's wisdom, and the weakness of God is stronger than man's strength. Brothers, think of what you were when you were called. Not many of you were wise by human standards; not many were influential; not many were of noble birth. But God chose the foolish things of the world to shame the wise; God chose the weak things of the world to shame the strong. He chose the lowly things of this world and the despised things—and the things that are not—to nullify the things that are, so that no one may boast before him.

"It is because of him that you are in Christ Jesus, who has become for us wisdom from God—that is, our righteousness, holiness and redemption. Therefore, as it is written: 'Let him who boasts boast in the Lord.'"

—1 Corinthians 1:17-31 NIV

So, you don't need to study deeply, to grasp all the details of history and prophecy. You just need to put your trust in Jesus as your Savior, and obey him as your Lord. Leave the rest to him. He will do the things he promised—to bless those who follow him, and to punish this corrupt world that rebels against God.

Many events related to the Middle East and the situation in Jerusalem will have transpired after the writing of this book. It is impossible for a book to be as up to date as the daily newspaper or the news service web sites that are updated hourly or even more frequently. And things do happen fast in times of conflict. But Bible prophecy was written thousands of years in advance, and is completely accurate—because it was written by the One "who from the very beginning foretold the future." (Isaiah 44:7 Jerusalem Bible) As the Apostle Peter wrote,

"No prophecy in the Scriptures ever comes from the prophet's own interpretation. No prophecy ever came from what a person wanted to say, but people led by the Holy Spirit spoke words from God."

—2 Peter 1:20-21 NCV

Some events may appear to be pushing things in the direction of fulfillment of Bible prophecy regarding Jerusalem and regarding the return of Christ. Other events may make things seem as if a different course will take place. Those who adhere to the Bible and keep their trust in God will be helped by his Holy Spirit to see beyond the confusion of apparently contradictory events. They will be able to see the true import of what is happening.

Political hopes for peace in the Middle East swing from optimistic to pessimistic and back again as fast as the ever changing events unfold on a daily basis. One week things seem to be heading in this direction, and the next week they seem to be heading in the opposite direction. But the consistent fulfillment of Bible prophecy down through history gives us confidence that events will finally move in the in the direction foretold in Scripture. And the observable events in the Middle East during the past hundred years reinforce that belief. The Balfour Declaration set the stage for the return of the Jews to the Promised Land. The restoration of the state of Israel in 1948 fulfilled prophecy and prepared the way for the final fulfillment.

A series of United Nations resolutions since 1947 declaring that Jerusalem must be an international city governed by the U.N. and under United Nations control set the stage for concerted action by all the nations against the state of Israel. And the growing power and authority of the United Nations as a loosely organized world government with an ever more active military arm during recent decades provides a final element needed to see the fulfillment of the prophecy of Zechariah, chapter twelve.

Since the radical Islamic terrorist attack against America on September 11, 2001, the status of Jerusalem is no longer merely a matter of local concern to the nations of the Middle East. Jerusalem has become a problem for the whole world, and all the nations are maneuvering to enforce their solution.

Jerusalem has become "a heavy stone burdening the world," as the ancient Hebrew prophet wrote, and "all the nations of the earth unite in an attempt" to impose their solution. (Zechariah 12:3 LB)

Meanwhile, the world around us has fallen into the condition of the world that provoked the flood of Noah's day, the world that provoked divine intervention at the tower of Babel, and the world that brought down fire and brimstone from Heaven in the days of Sodom and Gomorrah.

The days, months, and years ahead will see the return of the Jewish Messiah, Jesus Christ, the sudden rapture of his Church—the body of Christian believers—to join him in Heaven, and then God's final war, the battle of Armageddon.

Although the Bible contains all the details, we may not be able to puzzle them all out ahead of time. Yet, we can discern enough to trust that God knows exactly what will happen, and that he has declared what the final outcome will prove to be. Our job is to trust and obey.

By putting faith in God and his Messiah, we can face the frightening days ahead with joy and gladness instead of fear and terror. We can be sure that "the heathen will trample over Jerusalem" only "until their time is up." (Luke 21:20-24 TEV)

Jesus said,

"'When these things begin to take place, stand erect, hold your heads high, because your liberation is near at hand!'"

—Luke 21:28 Jerusalem Bible

Prophecy Timeline

EVENT	DATE	PROPHETIC TEXTS
Romans destroy temple and city of Jerusalem	**70 A.D.**	"When you see Jerusalem being surrounded by armies, you will know that its desolation is near. Then let those who are in Judea flee to the mountains, let those in the city get out, and let those in the country not enter the city. For this is the time of punishment in fulfillment of all that has been written. How dreadful it will be in those days for pregnant women and nursing mothers! There will be great distress in the land and wrath against this people."—Luke 21:20-23 NIV
The Jewish homeland ceases to exist, and the Jews are scattered worldwide	**70-135 A.D.**	"Then the LORD will scatter you among all nations, from one end of the earth to the other."—Deuteronomy 28:64 NIV "They will fall by the sword and will be taken as prisoners to all the nations. Jerusalem will be trampled on by the Gentiles until the times of the Gentiles are fulfilled."—Luke 21:24 NIV
Adolph Hitler's death camps exterminate millions of Jews over three and a half years.	**Dec. 1941 thru May 1945**	"When the end comes near for those kingdoms, a bold and cruel king . . . will cause terrible destruction and will . . . destroy . . . even God's holy people." "This king will speak against the Most High God, and he will hurt and kill God's holy people. . . . The holy people that belong to God will be in that king's power for three and one-half years." —Daniel 8:23-24; 7:25 NCV

EVENT	DATE	PROPHETIC TEXTS
Jews regain the Promised Land and establish the state of Israel	1948	"the LORD will . . . assemble the dispersed of Israel, and gather together the scattered of Judah from the four corners of the earth."—Isaiah 11:11-12 Jewish Publication Society of America

"Then the LORD your God will . . . bring you back again from the nations where he scattered you. . . . back to the land that belonged to your ancestors. It will be yours."—Deuteronomy 30:3-5 NCV |
| Jews take control of Jerusalem | 1967 | "Jerusalem will be trampled on by the Gentiles until the times of the Gentiles are fulfilled."—Luke 21:24 NIV |
| Men orbit the earth and land on the moon | Since the 1960s | "Immediately after the tribulation of those days . . . the powers of the heavens shall be shaken."—Matthew 24:29 KJV

". . . there shall be signs in the sun, and in the moon, and in the stars . . . for the powers of heaven shall be shaken."—Luke 21:25-26 KJV |
| Israel defeats Arab neighbors | 1967 until now | "Jerusalem a cup of trembling unto all the people round about" - Zech.12:2 KJV |
| Jerusalem a problem for the whole world | now | "Jerusalem will be a heavy stone burdening the world" — Zech.12:3 LB |
| The nations unite vs. Israel | soon | ". . . all the nations on earth will come together to attack Jerusalem."—Zechariah 12:3 NCV

"The armies of heaven . . . defeat the nations"—Revelation 19:14-15 NCV |

About the Writing of this Book

Anybody who writes a book on this subject is in danger of being compared to Aesop's fables' proverbial 'boy who cried wolf.' "Wolf! Wolf!" he shouted, to draw attention to himself, or to add some excitement to his life. People reacted just as he hoped they would. But then, on a later occasion when a wolf actually did appear on the scene—and he was in real danger—everyone assumed he was just 'crying wolf' again falsely. And no one came to his aid.

Similarly, there have been so many false alarms concerning the return of Christ and the end of the world, that most people laugh or shrug off any suggestion that the prophesied event will soon take place. And, when it comes to the matter of people "crying wolf" about the return of Christ, no one can be more painfully aware of it than I am. In 1968 I fell victim to the Watchtower Society's prediction that Armageddon would occur in the year 1975, and I spent the next thirteen years serving that organization—eight of those years as a Jehovah's Witness elder. By the time Bible reading eventually introduced me to the real Jesus and led me to embrace biblical Christianity in 1982, I was no longer interested in trying to understand the end times prophecies—other than to know that Christ would someday return.

Over the next twenty years or so, I authored a number of books exposing the failed prophecies and false teachings of the Jehovah's Witnesses and other sects, including *Jehovah's Witnesses Answered Verse by Verse* (1986, Baker Book House), *Answering Jehovah's Witnesses Subject by Subject* (1996, Baker Book House), *Mormons Answered Verse by Verse* (1992, Baker Book House), and *Blood on the Altar* (1996, Prometheus Books).

The horrific events of September 11, 2001, prompted me to look more closely at how current events were fulfilling end times prophecies—resulting in my creating a number of web sites on this topic. And in 2008 I produced the book *LEFT BEHIND Answered Verse by Verse*, which demonstrates how popular dispensationalist interpretations ignore the biblical insights of Luther, Calvin, Wesley, Tyndale, Knox and other great students of the Bible.

Our dear family friend Katie Tripp had been running off printed copies of one of my end times web sites to share with others, but then asked if I planned to put the material into book form. Actually, I hadn't. But her inquiry prompted me to collect that material together, update it, and assemble it together here.

So, this book is the product of decades of research on the topic of end times prophecy. But the book that I recommend most highly on this topic is the

Bible itself. Please don't read my books—or anyone else's—to the exclusion of reading the inspired Scriptures. Prayerfully reading the Bible itself is the best way to know and understand what God has said about the end of this world. And no one has summed it up better than the Apostle Peter, who expressed it this way:

"Dear friends, this is now my second letter to you. I have written both of them as reminders to stimulate you to wholesome thinking. I want you to recall the words spoken in the past by the holy prophets and the command given by our Lord and Savior through your apostles.

"Above all, you must understand that in the last days scoffers will come, scoffing and following their own evil desires. They will say, 'Where is this 'coming' he promised? Ever since our ancestors died, everything goes on as it has since the beginning of creation.' But they deliberately forget that long ago by God's word the heavens came into being and the earth was formed out of water and by water. By these waters also the world of that time was deluged and destroyed. By the same word the present heavens and earth are reserved for fire, being kept for the day of judgment and destruction of the ungodly.

"But do not forget this one thing, dear friends: With the Lord a day is like a thousand years, and a thousand years are like a day. The Lord is not slow in keeping his promise, as some understand slowness. Instead he is patient with you, not wanting anyone to perish, but everyone to come to repentance.

"But the day of the Lord will come like a thief. The heavens will disappear with a roar; the elements will be destroyed by fire, and the earth and everything done in it will be laid bare.

"Since everything will be destroyed in this way, what kind of people ought you to be? You ought to live holy and godly lives as you look forward to the day of God and speed its coming. That day will bring about the destruction of the heavens by fire, and the elements will melt in the heat. But in keeping with his promise we are looking forward to a new heaven and a new earth, where righteousness dwells.

"So then, dear friends, since you are looking forward to this, make every effort to be found spotless, blameless and at peace with him. Bear in mind that our Lord's patience means salvation, just as our dear brother Paul also wrote you with the wisdom that God gave him. He writes the same way in all his letters, speaking in them of these matters. His letters contain some things that are hard to understand, which ignorant and unstable people distort, as they do the other Scriptures, to their own destruction.

"Therefore, dear friends, since you have been forewarned, be on your guard so that you may not be carried away by the error of the lawless and fall from your secure position. But grow in the grace and knowledge of our Lord and Savior Jesus Christ. To him be glory both now and forever! Amen."

—2 Peter 3:1-18 NIV

Made in the USA
Charleston, SC
26 July 2013